Natural logic

Exploring Decision and Intuition

Mauro Maldonato • Silvia Dell'Orco

Translated by
Mark Weir

sussex
ACADEMIC
PRESS
Brighton • Portland • Toronto

2 4 6 8 10 9 7 5 3 1

First published in 2011 by
SUSSEX ACADEMIC PRESS
PO Box 139
Eastbourne BN24 9BP

and in the United States of America by
SUSSEX ACADEMIC PRESS
920 NE 58th Ave   Suite 300
Portland, Oregon 97213-3786

and in Canada by
SUSSEX ACADEMIC PRESS (CANADA)
90 Arnold Avenue, Thornhill, Ontario L4J 1B5

British Library Cataloguing in Publication Data
A CIP catalogue record for this book is available from the British Library.

Library of Congress Cataloging-in-Publication Data

Maldonato, Mauro.
  Natural logic : exploring decision and intuition / Mauro Maldonato and Silvia Dell'Orco ; translated by Mark Weir.
      p.   cm.
  Includes bibliographical references and index.
  ISBN 978-1-84519-484-0 (p/b : alk. paper)
  1. Decision making. 2. Intuition. 3. Logic. I. Dell'Orco, Silvia. II. Title.
  BF448.M357 2011
  160—dc23

                                        2011019191

Typeset and designed by Sussex Academic Press, Brighton & Eastbourne.
Printed by TJ International, Padstow, Cornwall.
This book is printed on acid-free paper.

Natural Logic

CONTENTS

INTRODUCTION

The evolution of the species has witnessed a rather unequal trade-off: while biology has given rise to culture, culture has not brought much of an improvement to human nature. Even if the human brain was rapidly endowed with a cortex, its sub-cortical structures (which are more closely related to the rhythms of nature) still conserve the same function as ever. Thus while it is true that the human mind has accumulated much information and knowledge by means of rational decisions, the vast majority of these decisions have been underpinned by a natural logic, with rules that have proved to be advantageous for our evolution.

There is now a large body of scientific evidence to disprove the theory that our mind is equipped with formal schemes of inference able to draw valid conclusions irrespective of the content of the premisses. During the 20th century the economic and psychological sciences highlighted the role of unpredictability and uncertainty in individual decision making. Herbert A. Simon was among the first to question the validity of the theory of normative rationality and clarify how, in conditions of uncertainty, it is contradicted by individuals' actual behaviour. The anti-normative nature of his theory was reflected – as we shall see in what follows – in the concept of *bounded rationality*, whereby cognitive limits oblige the decision maker to adopt simplified schemes in solving problems.

The decision-making process is heavily conditioned by distorted representations and perceptions of risk. Variables of this type, generated by chaotic, mobile and fluctuating factors, actually make optimal responses highly unlikely. Apart from the objective data available (statistics on difficulties, competitors, accidents and so on) there are also subjective and interpersonal factors influencing decisions: willingness to take and ability to assess risk, impact of the environment, fear for possible future consequences, personal courage, and so on. In most cases, decision makers do not dispose of sufficient information, statistical data or other relevant elements when assessing risk. Hence they rely on information and knowledge deriving from their direct experience, including prejudices, suppositions or deductions based on what they know at that moment in time, and the urgency of taking a decision, as well as what they remember, have heard or found out concerning the sources of risk.

The asymmetries between the models of rational choice and people's concrete behaviour can be explained by rules of rationality and informal choice criteria determined by the interference of cognitive and contextual elements in the assessment of the problem and the available information. Daniel Kahneman and Amon Tversky can undoubtedly claim credit for having recognised that choices are often sub-optimal because of the ways in which the problem is represented and the information is processed. Their research showed how people tend to envisage events not by objective calculation but according to structured memories or, if fear plays a part, authentic representations of conflict.

Experiments have shown that, in conditions of uncertainty, people reason as if they were dealing with certainties. As a matter of fact, in the case of models formulated to define the context or represent what appears to be true and not what appears to be false, alternative models are equivalent. In constructing mental models, decision makers concentrate on the explicit rather than the implicit information provided. This goes some way to explaining the oversights and distractions which can result in even serious accidents. In any decision, the activity of "focusing" on the problem can generate significant distortions. When called on to decide, most people focus on the variables in the plan of action, looking for confirmation rather than information about possible alternatives. Even in everyday life and situations involving trivial decisions (such as whether to buy one product or another, to go to the cinema or not), when confronted with one predominant option and in the absence of significant alternatives, there is a spontaneous tendency to focus, even though this contradicts the notion that, before choosing, a decision maker rationally examines the available options. In fact the example of focusing is extremely useful for understanding how the mind works with tools which have nothing to do with logico-formal attributes. And there is one further element to be taken into consideration. If, as we have seen, people (out of excessive confidence in their own judgement) tend to look for confirmation of their own ideas rather than for evidence to the contrary, this tendency diminishes when they are obliged to consider the pros and cons of an impending choice.

Statistical data are generally held to be objective, decisive elements in arriving at decisions concerning economics and other fields, while in fact they often prove to be fallacious and illusory. Considering statistics as snapshots of reality, reflecting the "bald facts" free of any subjective evaluation, can give rise to all sorts of problems. Not only do individual perceptions and judgements yield different results, but the average values and the preordained criteria hardly ever match up to a multiple, dynamic reality, and this certainly does not lend itself to representation using mathematical sets. In *How to lie with statistics* (1993) Darrell Huff argues that, far from "photographing" reality, statistical data tend to distort it. In his view the standard statistical procedures, which are supposed to provide a tool for living with uncertainty, actually create illusions of certainty, when not indeed groundless certainties. The figures hardly ever "speak for themselves": more often than not, they say what they are made to say. Thus it is essential to know how to "read" data to be able to decide in the various domains of human activity.

Is rationality a natural attribute of the human race? This is a dilemma which has been passed down through the centuries, and still confronts the scientific community today. Over the last 30 years a systematic analysis of human reasoning has come up with new and surprising answers. The questions traditionally posed by philosophers have given way to experimental investigations which, by analysing concrete cases which can be reproduced and verified, have contributed to clarifying a series of standard phenomena in our mental processes. People have been seen to unconsciously adopt rules that diverge from rationality. Moreover, this is not a reflex, psychological effect but a complex exercise achieved (and maintained) only at a specific psychological cost. The analysis of *biases* shows how cognitive illusions are indeed mere illusions, and ideal rationality nothing other than an ideal. The faculty of rationality is not innate to our species. Rather, we seem to be innately gifted at identifying certain contradictions, analysing and verifying them, and absorbing or rejecting them. The exercise of rationality obliges us to recognise our limits, to get to know better its haphazard geography, to elaborate new theories concerning the mind, and to improve our judgements.

But how are these natural limits and their function in our cognitive activity to be considered? While there can be no doubt that our knowledge has its biological roots in the brain, it is also certain that we are able to describe ourselves at a number of different levels. The biological and cognitive modalities intersect in the nervous system to produce that most familiar and elusive of all experiences: ourselves. Certainly we cannot go beyond the boundaries of ourselves or our mind. When we are pursuing a perception, an idea or a thought we have the sensation of being, as Francisco Varela put it on one occasion, in an «ever receding fractal». Whichever direction we take we inevitably find ourselves confronted with an enormous quantity of details and inter-relations, with no beginning or end.

Scientific opinion has fluctuated as to whether experience owes more to objective or subjective factors. But in terms of the natural history of the human mind, experience comes to be seen not as a postulate able to provide explanations but rather as the marker of a phenomenon of interaction in which subject and object are inextricably interwoven. It is impossible to identify where one begins and the other ends. Wherever one chooses to start, we are bound to find something which exactly mirrors the act we are performing. Such a mirroring does not tell us what the world is or is not like: it merely tells us that it is possible to be the way we are, and act the way we act.

This book about decision making envisages a new research programme able to redefine the role of external restrictions on human action and restore the due importance to the internal restrictions. The gradual recession of the (stressful) idea of a perfect rationality is making room for the (sustainable) idea of a perfectible and self-regulating rationality, aware of its own incompleteness and willing to confront what cannot be rationalised. In the various stages of writing we have often found ourselves thinking that another work is called for to clarify how the various topics discussed here inter-relate. For there is no unitary theory governing the research presented here. Knowledge, whether scientific or philosophical, can only claim to be such if it keeps issues open rather than closing them out. The way in which research is organized today tends all too often to foster hyper-specialization, making the object of study the be all and end all of scientific enquiry, and turning a scientific discipline into a watertight compartment which ignores the affinities and relations of its particular object with others. When this happens, disciplinary boundaries and linguistic and conceptual structures become instruments of separation that isolate one discipline from another. Whereas surely the growth of knowledge is enabled by overcoming disciplinary boundaries, by allowing concepts to circulate and new domains of knowledge to form. Contrary to the widely held belief that a notion pertains exclusively to the disciplinary field in which it originated, we are convinced that the most important ideas invariably show themselves to be fruitful in new fields which may even be quite remote from their birthplace.

In closing these brief introductory considerations we express the hope that we have contributed to clarifying some of the dynamics of decision making. Above all we hope we will encourage readers who set out to navigate through the extraordinary archipelago of rationality, mores, emotions and consciousness to take a new look at themselves and at human action in general.

UNDERSTANDING DECISION MAKING

Some Historical Remarks

Before entering the domain of the cognitive sciences, decision making –
one of the most mysterious and yet familiar topics of human reflection –
intrigued enquiring minds in every age and in the most disparate disci-
plines: philosophers, mathematicians, psychologists, economists and so
on. In the first attempts at researching the topic, dating as far back as the
Eleatic School, the investigation of human rationality pondered the
logical rules for exploring the validity of inferences and conclusions
starting from certain premises. In the *Nicomachean Ethics* Aristotle argued
that a decision is a "deliberate appetition" characterised by a logical and
psychological sequence which starts from desire, proceeds with will and
concludes with choice. During the Middle Ages, when the universe was
underpinned by religious orthodoxy, Scholasticism re-elaborated the
Aristotelian categories in an attempt to counter the orthodox denial of
both autonomous moral judgement and the individual exercise of free
choice. The growing confidence in modern rationality had a two-
pronged effect: on one hand it accelerated progress in empirical enquiry,
favouring the development of the experimental method and modern
science (viz. the discoveries of Copernicus, Galileo, Kepler, Newton); on
the other it tended to condemn the individual to an existence in which a
methodology based on hypothesis and deduction represented the only
possible means for understanding natural phenomena [Mirowski, 1989].

The progressive rationalisation of knowledge and human behaviour
had Descartes as its main protagonist. Writing in 1637, he asserted that
the mathematical sciences can benefit the whole field of human knowledge in both theoretical and empirical terms, if only the same
methodology is extended to other disciplinary spheres. The deductive

method guaranteed the rational certainty of an individual's existence against the delusion of sensible knowledge and the interference of emotive and affective factors. This was the origin of the philosophical dualism that has had such a great influence on the history of human thought. If in fact knowledge is the preserve of the mind, then the truth about things has necessarily to pass through the mind, rather than involving the mind and body together. External objects are perceived not through our senses – involving the complex activity of the talamus, receptors, spinal and cortical nerves and so on, as science has demonstrated during the 20th century – but exclusively through the intellect. It was no coincidence if Descartes considered perception an obscure function, deriving from the confused conjunction of mind and body and relying on the deceptive "knowledge" of the senses, notably seeing, touching and hearing. In these same years, across the English Channel, Hobbes was affirming that human choices are determined by the calculation of what is useful and what is harmful, while Locke went so far as to deny the universality and infallibility of reason. Not even the most rational individual, he claimed, can count on the clear light of certainty: his decisions are made amid the shadowy reflections of uncertainty. In an evocative image, he presented reason as a candle lighting us on our way, but casting too feeble a light to clarify everything in our path [Locke, 1690]. For Spinoza, decision making is merely an attribute of human thought, and free will is a desire for action which informs the desired objects.

Half way through the 18th century consideration of human rationality ventured beyond the exclusive terrain of philosophy and launched into new explorations, above all in the domain of economics. The publication of Adam Smith's *An Inquiry into the Causes of the Wealth of Nations* [1776] led to a profound schism in economic paradigms as economics parted ways with morality. Smith argued that not only is personal interest not harmful, but it is actually advantageous for society. In fact, in pursuing his own interest, each individual unintentionally also realises the good of the community. This gave rise to the famous metaphor of the invisible hand, which makes individual interests the basis of the public good:

> As every individual, therefore, endeavours as much as he can, both to employ his capital in the support of domestic industry, and so to direct that industry that its produce may be of the greatest value; every individual necessarily labours to render the annual revenue of the society as great as he can. He generally, indeed, neither intends to promote the public interest, nor knows how much he is promoting it. By preferring the support of domestic to that of foreign industry, he intends only his own security; and by directing that industry in such a manner as its produce may be of the greatest

value, he intends only his own gain, and he is in this, as in many other cases, led by an invisible hand to promote an end which was no part of his intention. [Smith, 1776, book IV, p. 184]

Smith maintained that even if its members do not love each other, a society can still thrive thanks to the advantages deriving from their reciprocal exchanges. His principle, expressed in the maxim "give me what I need and you will have what you require", lies at the heart of today's "free market". As a matter of fact, Bernard Mandeville [1714] had already stated that it is actually private vices, with the unintended effects of the initiatives they give rise to and the relative social benefits, which generate public virtues. Earlier still, Thomas Aquinus had written in *Summa Theologiae* that we "would be deprived of many advantages if all sins were strictly forbidden and punishments appointed for them" [ST 2-2.78.1.3] [*cited in* Letwin and Reynolds, 2005, p. 73]. In reality Smith was not the only advocate *ante litteram* of individualism and personal interest. The category of "sympathy" – which he defines as the ability of an individual to identify with a fellow creature – plays an essential role in his system of thought. Thus attempts to set Smith the economist against Smith the philosopher are surely wide of the mark. The theses he spelt out in *An Inquiry into the Causes of the Wealth of Nations* should be read in the light of, and not in contrast with, the ones expressed in *The Theory of Moral Sentiments* [1759]. In fact, if it is true that for Smith the pursuit of each individual's personal interests is bound to produce and increase the collective wealth, with the advantages being extended to one and all (albeit in different degrees), it is no less the case that there are certain principles in man's nature which spur him to consider others and care about their happiness [Smith, 1759]. In this connection we can recognise the importance of the distinction Smith makes between "self-interest" and "selfishness".

Unbounded Rationality and Expected Utility: The Birth of *Homo economicus*

Prior to the emergence of the cognitive sciences in the first half of the 20th century, the model for rational decision making drew on logic-mathematical schemes very similar to the advice Benjamin Franklin, himself a scientist as well as a statesman, gave his niece as she contemplated the prospect of marriage:

If you doubt, set down all the Reasons, pro and con, in opposite Columns on a Sheet of Paper, and when you have considered them two or three Days, perform an Operation similar to that in some questions of Algebra; observe what Reasons or Motives in each Column are equal in weight, one to one, one to two, two to three, or the like, and when you have struck out from both Sides all the Equalities, you will see in which column remains the Balance (. . .). This kind of Moral Algebra I have often practiced in important and dubious Concerns, and tho' it cannot be mathematically exact, I have found it extremely useful. By the way, if you do not learn it, I apprehend you will never be married. [Franklin, 1907, pp. 281–282]

Franklin's "moral algebra" is an intriguing metaphor for the theory of rational choice, whereby in order to choose the alternative with the greatest utility, individuals first consider all the consequences of each single action, then weigh them up, and lastly add up the pluses and minuses to obtain a final total. In this perspective, the choices and degrees of belief of a rational agent substantially correspond to the axioms of subjective or conditioned probability predicated in Bayes's theorem. Formulated in the mid-18th century by the mathematician and Presbyterian minister Thomas Bayes, it shows how to determine *a posteriori* the probability of a given hypothesis on the basis of its probability *a priori* and any relevant new information. Bayes's theorem constitutes not only a normative reference concerning how to draw the correct conclusions about the probabilities *a posteriori* of a given event, but also the chief point of reference for almost all methods for treating uncertain knowledge [Shafer and Pearl, 1990].

It can be expressed in the following formula: given a hypothesis H and the event E, the probability *a posteriori* of the hypothesis H is calculated as:

$$p\,(H/E) = \frac{p\,(E/H) \cdot p\,(H)}{p\,(E)}$$

WHERE

- $p\,(H/E)$ is the probability *a posteriori* that, given the event E, the hypothesis H is true;
- $p\,(E/H)$ is the probability *a priori* of the event E, if the hypothesis H is true;
- $p\,(H)$ is the probability *a priori* (or "base probability") of the hypothesis H;
- $p\,(E)$ is the probability *a priori* of the event E

For example, let us suppose that the incidence of an illness in the population is 1 case in 1,000,000. Let us further suppose that the test is not always reliable, and gives a positive result in 5% of cases in which the person tested has not contracted the illness. What is the probability that a person who has tested positive actually has the illness?

IN THIS CASE:

$$p\ (H) = \frac{1}{1\ 000\ 000}$$

is the probability *a priori* of the hypothesis H (the person has the illness), meaning that one person selected at random among the population has the illness;

- $p\ (E/H) = 1$

is the probability that the test gives a positive result when the illness is present; and

- $p\ (E) = 1 \cdot 0.000001 + 0.05 \cdot 0.999999 = 0.05$

is the probability that the event E will occur, calculated as the sum of the probabilities that the event will occur respectively in the case of a sick and a healthy person, taking into account the base probability that a person is either sick or healthy and the result of the test in both cases. APPLYING BAYES'S THEOREM WE GET:

$$p\ (H/E) = \frac{1 \cdot 0.000001}{0.05}$$

In other words, given a positive test, the probability that the person actually has the illness is equivalent to 0.002%. Individuals can thus always take a rational approach to uncertainty, using what for De Finetti constitutes "the lynchpin and fundamental concept of every constructive mental activity" [1970, p. 156]. The theory of rational choice found a propitious terrain in Utilitarianism which, in the second half of the 18th century, focused on the hierarchy of preferences or the "utility function". Jeremy Bentham defined utility as whatever produces happiness, minimising pain and maximising pleasure. It is a hedonistic calculus, positing that everything which corresponds to utility goes to increase well-being, making it the philosophical equivalent of Franklin's moral algebra. According to Bentham, society is an aggregate of individual interests governed by an instrumental rationality which identifies the most suitable means for achieving certain ends. In this sense pursuit of individual utility involves, on the larger scale, the increase of social well-being, and this substantiates the moral and social value of what is useful.

In 1738 the Swiss mathematician Daniel Bernoulli introduced a concept which was to prove fundamental in the theory of individual decision making. It formed part of the solution he proposed to the Saint Petersburg paradox, formulated 25 years earlier by his cousin Nicolas, which in its most general form runs as follows. The clients of a Saint Petersburg casino were entitled to gamble on payment of a fixed entrance fee. If for example a gambler bet correctly that the first throw of a coin would produce heads, he would double his stake. According to the traditional theory of *expected value*, a gambler should always participate in such a game of chance, whatever the stake, since the expected value is infinite (at each throw the winnings double, although the probability of obtaining them halves). However, Bernoulli, who had plenty of opportunity to observe the gambling at the court of Peter the Great, noticed that most people are not willing to pay out high sums to play, and above all, no one is willing to commit himself to an infinite sum. Thus the criterion of expected value proves to be inadequate to explain the decisions made in real life.

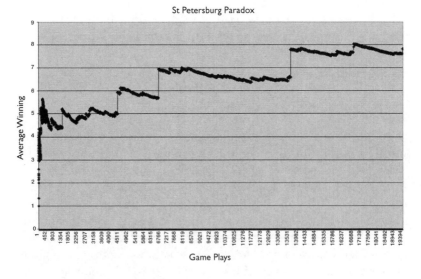

Figure I In the graph the average worth of winnings is plotted against the number of plays. Initially large winnings are matched by significant increases in value; the worth decreases in correspondence to small winnings, and goes up again at the next large win. Although the average worth of the winnings tends to increase to infinity, this is actually an extremely slow process: after nearly 20,000 plays it is approximately equivalent to 8.

In the solution Bernoulli proposed for the paradox, the concept of *expected value* (objective value) was replaced by *expected utility* (subjective or psychological value). He argued that the determination of the value of an object cannot be based on its intrinsic advantages but merely on the utility it procures. The object's advantages depend solely on the object itself, and are the same for everybody, whereas its utility depends on the person making the evaluation. Clearly 1000 ducats mean much more to a poor man than to a rich man, even though the economic gain is the same for both [Bernoulli, 1738]. Thus the price of a good depends only on the article in question and is the same for everyone, while its utility will be evaluated differently by each individual, because it depends on subjective circumstances (such as the urgency of the need for that good, the quantity already owned, and so on). Moreover Bernoulli specified that the *expected utility* of an increase in wealth (meaning in the goods owned) increases as this goes up, but in inverse proportion to the quantity owned. In economic terms this is described as *diminishing marginal utility*.

Bernoulli's intuition marked the beginning of the marginalist

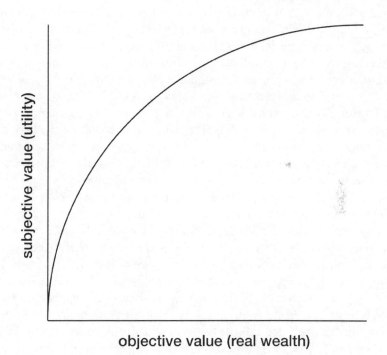

objective value (real wealth)

Figure 2 The classic subjective utility function. The horizontal axis shows the objective or real wealth possessed by the subject; the vertical axis shows the subjective value or utility attributed to that wealth. The utility of monetary gains tends towards saturation level: the curve flattens out as the winnings increase.

revolution, a key moment in the emergence of the neoclassical theoretical system based on the notions of utility and material self-interest developed by Jevons [1871], Menger [1871] and Walras [1874]. Marginalism favoured the development of methodological individualism in contrast to the social historical analysis of classical economics. With the neoclassical theory the concept of rationality took on normative connotations and the economic process focused on the individual optimisation of the scarce means available for alternative uses [Robbins, 1932]. Of course, one has to consider the cultural context (imbued with positivism and scientism) surrounding this development. The science of economics was striving to conform as closely as possible to the epistemic status of the natural sciences, universally recognised as science *par excellence*. The value attributed to the great scientific advances in the 17th and 18th centuries reinforced the conviction that the best recipe for success consisted in adopting the method used in physics and mathematics. The prestige of the Newtonian (or pseudo-Newtonian) model was so overwhelming that nobody dared to query the axiom that order and harmony were in some way produced by human atoms acting according to their nature, whether the instinct for play and pleasure or the egoistic pursuit of gain [Koyré, 1968]. Adopting the methodology of physics and mathematics, it became inevitable to consider individual and social behaviour as tending to a state of equilibrium. This concept, closely bound up with that of *utility*, represents another significant aspect of the "mathematization" of the social sciences. Attempts to explain the concept of equilibrium in economics have involved a number of analogies with physics and mechanics, including: the swing of a pendulum; the periodical motion of a heavenly body round a fixed point; hydrodynamics [Canard, 1801], whereby an economic system is endowed, like the human body, with homeostatic and self-regulatory functions; or again the parallel with the forces operating on each end of a pair of scales. Léon Walras sought to construct an authentic science of economic forces by analogy with statics (the science of the equilibrium of bodies) and with the dynamics of the heavenly bodies. His theory of general economic equilibrium, set out in *Eléments d'économie politique pure* [1900], stood as a sort of *magna charta* for economic theory up until the mid-twentieth century [Schumpeter, 1939]. He maintained that once a "mechanics of moral forces" was in place, "the law of man's behaviour will be scientifically established as is the law of the Earth's movement around the sun" [Walras, 1936, p. vii]. However, this analogy required the existence of a fundamental law governing the economy with the same functions as Newton's law of gravity, a general principle from which all other laws could be derived as simple corollaries. The principle underlying all the laws and mechanisms in economics had been identified as self-interest

[Edgeworth, 1881; Jevons, 1871; Pantaleoni, 1889]. Walras's main contribution was to combine equations relating to equilibrium adopted from statics with a theory of value based on marginal utility. The value of a commodity is determined by its rarity or subjective scarcity (*rareté*), occurring when the demand for that article is greater than its availability. From his father August he assimilated the idea that value is the only conceivable type of measurement in the sciences in general, and in political economics in particular [A. Walras, 1831].

The transition from the classical theory of value based on production and distribution formulated by Adam Smith, Ricardo and Marx to its neoclassical counterpart, based on exchange, led to a change of focus in economics, from problems of development and economic growth to the allocation of resources. The idea that a social system driven by independent actions in the pursuit of different values is coherent with an end state of equilibrium is one of the most important contributions that the discipline of economics has made to the comprehension of social processes [Arrow and Hann, 1971]. The fundamental insight expressed by Adam Smith with the image of the invisible hand [Ingrao and Israel, 1990] was identified by Walras in the "law of supply and demand", by which if demand exceeds supply, the price of goods rises, while if supply exceeds demand, their price falls. In the preface to the fourth edition of the *Eléments* [1900], Walras argued that political economics is the theory of the determination of prices in a system of absolutely free competition [Walras, 1900]. This means that to make a rigorous calculation of the exchange value, the economic system must be inscribed in an ideal context of perfect competition. This is usually the case in an auction, a static, deterministic and timeless system in which individual market behaviour is described by a utility function and the initial amount of goods belonging to each individual. In their classic *Theory of Games and Economic Behaviour* [1947], Neumann and Morgenstern criticised Walras's theory of equilibrium for ignoring the interactions between the various subjects and the influence this has on individual decisions. A "new mathematics" was called for, and "games theory" appeared the best solution. Thus the classical approach was turned upside down: economic processes are not independent actions carried out by agents capable of making perfect predictions, but games involving multiple interactions which have unpredictable influences on the decisions of each agent. In this sense, if individuals possess partial information on the "economic game" in which they are involved, there is a need for probabilistic calculations which will make it possible, albeit with margins of error, to foresee the adversary's moves and choose a rational strategy. Neumann and Morgenstern provided the economic theory with the "normative" grounding of a rigorous, axiomatic science endowed with formal

4 UNDERSTANDING DECISION MAKING

elegance, free from the constrictions of the decision maker. They formulated a set of axioms underwriting the Expected Utility (EU) theory by which maximising utility represents a "rational" decision-making approach between risky alternatives [Oliverio, 2007]. Since the consequences of almost all our choices are uncertain, the theory of decision making portrays the objects of individual choice as "lotteries" or "probabilistic prospects". For example, in the case of a binary lottery there is a real utility function U whereby X will be preferred to Y if and only if the EU of X is greater than the EU of Y:

$$X > Y <\downarrow\downarrow> EU\ (X) > EU\ (Y)$$

According to the normative model, a rational decision will be based on formal criteria and coherences expressed by means of a rigorous sequence of axiomatic demonstrations which represent, more than a mode, a genuine paradigm [Hogarth and Reder, 1986]. Among the principal axioms in the theory of EU there are:

- Axiom of transitivity: if result A is preferred to result B and B is preferred to C, then result A must be preferred to result C;
- Axiom of dominance: if option A is more advantageous than option B in all of the possible configurations, then one must prefer option A to option B regardless of the present configuration;
- Axiom of invariance: the order of preferences cannot be modified or overturned by the way in which the options are proposed. In other words, the decision must be insensitive to the variations in the presentation of the decision-making problem;
- Axiom of independence: if there is a condition that leads to the same result irrespective of the choice made, then the choice must not depend on that result [Savage, 1954]. In other words, if an individual prefers one action over another, he must not be influenced by the degree of uncertainty of events.

To provide a theoretical legitimation of the optimisation hypothesis, Alchian [1950] and Friedman [1953] both used Darwinian metaphors. Just as those species which best adapt to a given environment are most successful in surviving and reproducing, so in economic terms it is the agent who can optimise his decisions who survives best: all the others will inevitably drop out of the market because they are less able to adapt. In this perspective, the individual maximalisation of the EU represents a normative criterion which describes the ideal attitude of an economic agent who has to decide between risky alternatives. The attitude of the decision maker may be neutral, averse to or in favour of risk. For example, in the case of opting for heads or tails, if the subject is neutral with respect to risk he will be indifferent to whether he gambles or not (a linear preference function). If he is averse to risk, the EU diminishes as the sum at stake rises: maximising the EU implies not gambling (a convex utility function). Finally, if the subject favours risk, the EU increases as the sum at stake rises, and maximising the EU implies staking the highest sum possible (a concave utility function). Although it is coherent with the normative theories of rationality, aversion to risk does not represent the rule (as Kahneman and Tversky were to demonstrate), since it would not account for the widespread phenomenon of gambling involving high risk behaviour.

The Decline of Laplacian Rationality

According to normative rationality, it is possible to describe human decision-making behaviour by means of straightforward mathematical axioms. In other words, whether we are talking about the motion of the planets or human behaviour, everything can be described in terms of cause and effect through a mathematical representation of the phenomena. This interpretation of the world using mathematical principles has characterised mechanistic philosophies of nature for three centuries, but in the wake of positivism it is has expanded to cover social, economic and political phenomena. The most radical exponent of this approach was the French philosopher and physicist Pierre-Simon Laplace. In the introduction to *Essai philosophique des probabilités* [1825] he observed that if an intelligence which at a given moment knew all the forces acting in nature and the respective situation of the participatory agents were so vast as to be able to analyse all these data, it would be able to embrace in one and the same formula the motions of the largest bodies in the universe and of the most insignificant atom. Nothing would be uncertain: both the future and the past would be readily apparent. In the excellence achieved in the science of astronomy, the human mind has attained a pale imitation of this intelligence. The progress made in mechanics and geometry, together with the discovery of the law of gravity, have enabled scientists to devise analytic formulae which reveal the past and future states of systems in our world. By applying the same method to other objects of human knowledge, they have succeeded in reducing observed phenomena to general laws and foreseeing what will happen in given circumstances. All these efforts in the pursuit of truth tend to bring humans constantly closer to the intelligence posited by Laplace, yet they are doomed to remain infinitely far from achieving it.

Without any doubt, the regularity that astronomy shows us in the movements of the comets takes place in all phenomena. The trajectory of a simple molecule of air or vapour is regulated in a manner as certain as that of the planetary orbits; the only difference between them is that which is contributed by our ignorance. Probability is relative in part to this ignorance, and in part to our knowledge. [Laplace, 1825; Eng. tr. 1995, p. 3]

Laplace was in fact evoking a superhuman intelligence – "Laplace's demon" – which is able to know, even just for an instant, the position and degree of motion of each single particle in the universe, calculating all events in the cosmos, whether past, present or future. In this universe, nature is governed from the outset by rigid causal laws which are reflected in the mathematical equations that describe it. It is not a matter of the exact predictability of natural phenomena but of their accessibility to an intelligence which is immeasurably larger than human intelligence. Although the behaviour of *homo economicus* is guided by a rigorous rationality, it appears far removed from that of an actual individual. Thus representing reasoning and choices in terms of maximising the EU is like explaining a complex physical system with a simple formula. The variables involved are so numerous, and based on so few measurable paradigms, that any such attempt is doomed to fail [Tsebelis, 1990]. But is it really the pursuit of maximum utility which makes us take a decision, or are we also influenced by experience, emotions, our personal history and the way in which the problems are posed? What part is played by subjectivity, free will, desire or culture? It is these critical issues which make the theory of rational choice problematic, rather than the formal requisites of its utility functions. The contexts in which the decision maker is called on to choose have been overlooked, and one historical fact ignored. In the lengthy process of adaptation to a highly complex and unpredictable world, our forefathers relied for their survival on things which had nothing to do with normative axioms, artificial syntaxes and formal logic [Maldonato, 2010]. In actual fact, the first criticisms of *homo economicus* came from economists. As we mentioned above, one of the axioms that underlie the theory of EU is known as the axiom of independence: if an individual prefers A to B (A>B), C should be preferred to D (C>D) without being influenced by the degree of uncertainty in the events. According to Allais [1953], the perception of risk is distorted by numerous psychological factors not contemplated by Neumann and Morgenstern's model. He demonstrated the violation of the axiom of independence with the following example. For three possible money prizes – 500 million francs, 100 million francs and 0 francs – there are two independent choices: the first between A and B, the second between C and D.

Most of the subjects in the experiment contravened the axiom of inde-

A	C
Certainty of receiving 100 million	11 possibilities out of 100 to win 100 million 89 possibilities out of 100 not to win anything
B	B
10 possibilities out of 100 to win 500 million 89 possibilities out of 100 to win 100 million 1 possibility out of 100 not to win anything	10 possibilities out of 100 to win 500 million 90 possibilities out of 100 not to win anything

Figure 3 Allais's Paradox

pendence by preferring A to B in the first case and D to C in the second. The first choice showed that the certainty of receiving 100 million was preferable to entering a lottery offering 5 times that sum with a probability of 1:10, when in any case one risked receiving nothing at all. On the contrary, the second choice showed that winning 500 million with a probability of 1:10 was preferable to winning only 100 million with a probability that was only slightly less (11:100). According to the axiom of independence, if A is preferred to B, then C should be preferred to D, but here this did not happen. We can clarify this point by considering the respective EU [Oliverio, 2007]:

The first choice (A>B) equals: $.11U(100)>.10U(500)$
The second choice (D>C) equals: $.10U(500)>.11U(100)$
The two results $.11U(100)>.10U(500)$ and $.10U(500)>.11U(100)$ are contradictory and thus violate the axiom of independence.

Subsequently Ellsberg [1961] presented another experiment which also cast doubt on the ability of the EU model to define individual behaviour in making choices in conditions of uncertainty. Whereas Allais's experiment took place in a context where the probabilities were known, Ellsberg's dealt with unknown probabilities. Participants were confronted with two problems.

EXPERIMENT 1. Two urns, A and B, each contain 100 balls. Urn A contains 50 red balls and 50 black balls; urn B contains red and black balls in unknown proportions (it could contain 0 black balls and 100 red balls, 1 black ball and 99 red, 99 black and 1 red, etc.). One ball is extracted from the chosen urn at random (the participant is blindfolded). A red ball wins a prize X, a black ball nothing. From which urn would you prefer to extract a ball?

EXPERIMENT 2. With the same urns, participants are once again asked to express their preference as to which urn to extract a ball from. Now, however, it is a black ball that wins the prize.

In most cases the preferences were as follows:

Experiment 1: alternative A was preferred to B.
Experiment 2: alternative A was preferred to B.

Most of the subjects involved in the experiment felt there was a better chance of extracting a red ball from urn A. In reality in urn B too the probability of extracting a red or a black ball is 50%. The rational response is that, in both experiments, we should be indifferent to the choice of urn from which to extract a ball. Our decisions should in fact be governed only by the probability of making a winning. This paradox shows how usually we tend to "avoid the worst", a phenomenon described in the literature as aversion to ambiguity [Bowen, Qiu and Li, 1994; Curley, Yates and Abrams, 1986]. At the same time as Allais was publishing his experiments, criticisms of the notion of neoclassical rationality – and the informational, computational and cognitive limits of its model of the decision maker – came from a research group based at the Carnegie Mellon School which included such scholars as Simon (Nobel prize winner for economics in 1978), Cyert, March and Guetzkow. The analysis of the decision-making behaviour of managers in industry showed how, rather than pursue optimal and maximising solutions, they look for strategies which satisfy certain levels of aspirations (goals) and criteria of adequacy ("good enough"). Theory concerning decision making was still in its infancy. However prophetic it was, Weber's analysis of rational behaviour and the progressive bureaucratisation of society, expressed in terms of neoclassical economics, failed to take into account managers' behaviour, although in fact they are constantly in search of solutions to specific problems and have to innovate in situations in continuous flux. The traditional approach was to study the contexts of decisions and look for more appropriate strategies. In *Economy and Society* [1954] Weber argued that rational behaviour involves acting in accordance with one's objective, taking rational measurements of the means with respect to the ends and the possible goals in terms of their reciprocity. Shortly thereafter Simon [1957] put forward a theory of human choice which contemplated not only the rational aspects, the natural object of enquiry for economics, but also the ambiguities and limits, which he then set about investigating. If *Homo economicus* was an optimising animal, Simon's actor was a "satisficing" animal (his own neologism, meaning at once satisfying and sufficing) which looks for solutions that meet its preferences and goals through a process of research rather than deductive reasoning.

> The model of rational man put forward makes three exceedingly important demands upon the choice-making mechanism. It assumes (1) that all alternatives of choice are "given"; (2) that all the consequences attached to each alternative are known (in one of the three senses corresponding to certainty, risk, and uncertainty respectively); (3) that the rational man has a complete utility-ordering (or cardinal function) for all possible sets of consequences. [March and Simon, 1958, p. 138]

In view of their cognitive limits, decision makers adopt heuristic rules of behaviour which make it possible to simplify their decision-making models and at the same time to coordinate with the other agents to reduce the degree of uncertainty in complex economic systems. In this sense the organization is a system deriving from the interaction between individual components which take coordinated and cooperative decisions, solving problems on the basis of information and representations of the external environment. To do this it is necessary not only to look for the relevant information but also to construct a "mental model" which can represent the decision-making context as realistically as possible. With the concept of bounded rationality Simon [1979] incorporates both these dynamics of decision making, showing that the true constriction on a rational choice is the context, not the lack of information. Often, in fact, decision makers operate with excess information which is difficult to take into consideration and evaluate. These cognitive – but also ethical, cultural, emotive and social – limitations give rise to factors of uncertainty and ambiguity which influence their decisions. Developing Simon's theses, Heiner [1983] pointed out that alternative choices and the relative consequences are hardly ever clearly defined, and this is already enough to weaken the logical structure of the theory of optimisation. He coined the term "competence difficulty gap" for the irreconcilable dichotomy between the competence of agents (i.e. the set of skills which they use in problem solving) and the difficulty of choosing the optimal behaviour. One of Heiner's best known examples features Rubik's cube, a puzzle based on complete information which can be solved starting from billions of possible starting positions. In principle, when an agent endowed with "unlimited" rationality observes the initial pattern on the faces of the cube [Hodgson, 1991], he should recognise the information needed to choose the fastest solution. However, the cognitive limits of agents, together with the difficulties in solving the puzzle, do not consent an optimal solution. As Heiner himself remarked, there are sub-optimal techniques which make it possible to arrive at the solution irrespective of the starting position. Furthermore, while neoclassical theory views information as a negotiable commodity in short supply, just like any generic commodity or production factor, several authors [Marschak and Radner, 1972; Hey, 1979] have shown that not only is it limited but that, in conditions of excess, it could actually fail to be perceived and processed by the decision makers. Excess, complexity, heterogeneity and limited capacity to interpret the information call into question the neoclassical analysis of information put forward by Stigler [1961], who maintained it could be evaluated in terms of cost benefits. Since incoherence of expectations and cognitive incompleteness – generated by the scarcity or excess of information to be processed – characterise the most diverse contexts of individual choice, the decision maker will have to adapt to flexible conditions employing learning operations which reduce the complexity of the calculations required for the decision. In the descriptive approach to decision making, the choices performed by individuals are determined not only by some complete and coherent objectives and by the properties of the external world but also by the knowledge which decision makers possess – or do not possess – concerning the world, their ability or inability to call up such knowledge at the appropriate moment, to deal with the consequences of their actions, to predict the possible course of events, to tackle uncertainties (including those deriving from the possible reactions or responses of other agents) and to choose among the various competing needs [Simon, 1997]. In the mid-20th century, while many economists went along with Friedman's "as if" doctrine [1953] – according to which people behave "as if" they were indeed able to carry out the complex calculations required by the normative model – Simon opened up a new perspective in psychological and economic reflections on rationality by highlighting the paradoxes and anomalies in human behaviour. Simon's ideas paved the way for a large number of experiments into the "deviations" of individual behaviour from what neoclassical economic theory led one to expect. His research was felicitously pursued by Kahneman and Tversky, who showed conclusively that such deviations are systematic and not casual. In his acceptance speech for the Nobel prize for economics in 1978, Simon cited numerous economists who had contributed to establishing the theoretical grounding for bounded rationality. Among them he included Hayek, who argued that both the mental order that underlies the elaboration of individual choice and the context in which individuals are called on to choose are considerably more complex than is recognised under the neoclassical theory of rationality. But we shall come on to this later.

2

ECONOMICS VERSUS COGNITIVE SCIENCES

Towards an Integrated Theory of Human Decision Making

Hayek and the Birth of Evolutionary Rationalism

Friedrich von Hayek, one of the most eminent exponents of the Austrian School and winner of the Nobel prize for economics in 1974, was an intransigent critic of the neoclassical economic theory. From his début article entitled *Economics and Knowledge* [1937], his research made a decisive break with the concept of equilibrium and abstract rationality. He argued that rationality is based on a conscious gnoseological fallibility and the dynamism of individual action, and was convinced that the "fatal presumption" of neoclassical rationality derived from Descartes's constructivist approach.

> Descartes maintained that all of the useful human institutions were, and should be, the deliberate creation of conscious reason (. . . [denoting] . . .) an ability of the mind to arrive at the truth through a deductive process of few obvious and indubitable premises. [1967, p. 85]

Whereas according to Hayek, man is incapable not only of arriving at the truth by means of logico-formal deductions but also of controlling his own destiny because his own reason is continually progressing, leading him into the unknown and unforeseeable [Hayek, 1994]. Hayek believed that the economy is autonomous with respect to the exact sciences. Economic phenomena – continually subject to the unpredictable shifts of individual interactions – cannot be reduced to deductive inferences. Thus human activity is unpredictable because it is based on heterogeneous goals leading into different paths than the ones intended. He felt we should return to Adam Smith and the distinction made by the Ancient Greeks between *taxis* (constructed order) and *cosmos* (spontaneous order). Order in human affairs is the outcome not of a deliberate human project (*taxis*) but of a spontaneous order (*cosmos*) [Hayek, 1973]. As he points out, the "invisible hand" posited by Smith is a metaphor designed to represent the interactions of economic agents in the free market where each individual, motivated purely by self-interest, achieves the greatest possible interest for the collectivity. Most of the time human beings, without any rational overall project to guide them, try to deal with recurrent problems by setting up institutions designed to solve them in the best way possible. Instead human reason should recognise its own limits and consider that a spontaneous order – meaning an order generated without an overall design – can go well beyond anything achieved by deliberate effort. In this sense an economic decision is never the outcome of given alternatives but rather of a process of creation and individual elaboration independent of any deliberate planning [Hayek, 1952].

> The premise for this theory lies in the partiality and fallibility of human knowledge and in the awareness that the value of objects is not intrinsic and self-evident but is subjectively attributed by individuals. Abstract rationalism, on the contrary, claims that agents possess information in a much greater degree than can possibly be elaborated by the human mind. However, such omniscience would transform economics «into a branch of pure logic, a set of self-evident propositions which, like mathematics or geometry, are subject to no other test but internal consistency». [Hayek, 1937, pp. 33–34]

Borrowing the concepts of evolution and the spontaneous order of society and institutions from Bernard Mandeville's *The Fable of the Bees* [1714], Hayek reproposes the idea that individual actions, even when motivated by the most egoistic objectives, have positive consequences for the community. In *The Sensory Order* [1952], one of the most acute contributions cognitive psychology has made to classical economic theory [Rizzello, 1997], the strong psychological component of Hayek's individualism emerges in all its clarity. Hayek is convinced that in order to understand the dynamics of individual decision making one has to investigate the limits of the mind and consider the evidence provided by neurophysiology and psychology. Anticipating the major advances made in the neurosciences [Fuster, 1997; Paller, 2001], he tried to link the qualitative dimensions of perception to the activity of the brain, analysing in particular the process by which these dimensions are transformed into personal knowledge. The human mind, Hayek affirmed, is a *framework* containing a set of guiding *patterns* which, on the basis of previous experiences, give order to our world view, operating gradual and continuous adjustments in response to environmental stimuli. According to Hayek, «[. . .] mental events are a particular order of physical events within a subsystem of the physical world that relates the larger subsystem of the physical world that we call an organism (and of which they are part) with the whole system so as to enable the organism to survive» [Hayek, 1982, p. 288].

In this series of events – regulated by selection and creation within the brain, subsequently transformed into epigenetic traces in a species-characteristic process – sensorial inputs are continuously being remodelled on the basis of meta-conscious and pre-sensorial dynamics deriving from subjective experiences and neuronal connexions. Such processes become rooted in the course of an individual's personal history through organic links with the physical, social and cultural environment, and ultimately contribute to the evolution of the species. Thanks to recent studies of the nervous system we now know that neuronal circuits and cerebral structures, designed to interact with the external reality, are continually being modified and evolve in directions which can only partly be foreseen and predetermined. This process underpins an implicit, unconscious knowledge – on a different level to the traditional concept of cognition – which cannot be either known or communicated explicitly [Polanyi, 1951] because it is too elevated for the human mind.

In Hayek's model individual action derives from a dual knowledge: one conscious and the other unconscious. Thus the decision maker has to cope with a complex set of factors which are not contemplated by the rigid constrictions of traditional logic, making errors of judgement – that may even be substantial – inevitable. While classical economists attribute the imperfect interpretation of external signals to individual errors, Hayek ascribes these errors to the ways in which knowledge is constructed. In fact, while it is true that agents receive or acquire information, it is equally true that they operate on the basis of a knowledge that is the result of the elaboration – through tacit, personal and often idiosyncratic mechanisms – of that same information. Hayek describes a highly *path-dependent* process of knowledge formation because it is conditioned by the history, genetic characteristics and above all the experience, both conscious and meta-conscious, of each individual. It is this that leads Hayek to maintain that «human decisions must always appear as the result of the whole of human personality – that means the whole of a person's mind – which, as we have seen, we cannot reduce to something else» [1952; p. 193].

The empirical and predictive fragility of normative theories with respect to the actual dynamics of decision making became more and more apparent in the second half of the 20th century. The idea of a normative or instrumental rationality fell out of favour because it proved incompatible with everyday decision making and behaviour. Although consumer conditioning generates market behaviour that is in many cases close to the conventional model, when consumers are asked direct or unconventional questions concerning their habits or values, there is a marked divergence from the conventional rational models of economists [McFadden, 2005].

Simon and the Concept of Bounded Rationality

A crucial element in Simon's research is the concept of *bounded rationality* [Simon, 1979], whereby subjects' cognitive-computational abilities find no match in the *rational choice* of neoclassical economics. In a theoretical advance which disconcerted most economists, Simon called for reform of the science of economics by exposing it to contamination from other spheres of knowledge (primarily cognitive psychology) and above all by placing the fallibility of the decision maker at the heart of theoretical and empirical economics. One might say that Simon's research consists primarily in investigating the limits of human nature. His descriptive or behavioural approach to studying decisions of the *grounded-in-reality* type is based on observation rather than axioms or a priori principles and statements [Berthoz, 2006].

> The classical model calls for knowledge of all the alternatives that are open to choice. It calls for complete knowledge of, or ability to compute, the consequences that will follow on each of the alternatives. It calls for certainty in the decision maker's present and future evaluation of these consequences. It calls for the ability to compare consequences, no matter how diverse and heterogeneous, in terms of some consistent measure of utility. The task, then, was to replace the classical model with one that would describe how decisions could [and probably actually were] made when the alternatives of search had to be sought out, the consequences of choosing particular alternatives were only imperfectly known both because of uncertainty in the external world, and the decision maker did not possess a general and consistent utility function for comparing heterogeneous alternatives. [Simon, 1979, p. 500]

Ignoring the effective capacity for calculation and the human limits of rationality would be like «omitting gravitational forces from astrophysical theory» [Simon, 1997, p. 319]. The ability of the human mind to solve complex problems is very limited when compared to the quantity of problems to be tackled and overcome [Rumiati and Bonini, 1992]. In fact the real world is made up of a set of chaotic and ambiguous data which do not lend themselves to logico-deductive inferences. To act involves necessarily making do with incomplete information, time constraints and limited computational possibilities. Simon's focus on the decision-making process rather than the outcome of choice has paved the way for studying how decision makers acquire information about the world, re-elaborate it and finally make use of it to formulate their choices.

Simon argued that the limited rationality of an economic agent is manifested in the inability of its "internal environment" (the limits of cognition and computation) to process all the information and signals coming from the "external environment" [Simon, 1957], making it impossible to formulate an optimal choice. In other words, the limits of rationality derive from the

> [...] inability of the human mind to bring to bear upon a single decision all the aspects of value, knowledge, and behavior that would be relevant. The pattern of human choice is often more a stimulus-response pattern than a choice among alternatives. Human rationality operates, then, within the limits of a psychological environment". [Simon 1957, p. 108]

Behavioral economics, which grew out of Simon's research, attempts to integrate the classical theory of rational choice with new hypotheses adopted from psychology, and in particular experimental psychology [Mullainathan and Thaler, 2000], shifting the focus from substantive to procedural rationality. *Searching and satisficing* [Simon, 1978] are the key words in a decision-making process based on bounded rationality: agents review the available alternatives in succession and stop when their search reaches a specific or implicit threshold of satisfaction, which does not correspond to an optimal solution. An individual faced with an economic decision behaves like a chess player considering the next move. Both follow certain procedures: the winning strategy is constructed by degrees, not a priori, in the manner of a tree diagram, and is constantly open to reconsideration in view of the opponent's moves. Moreover, in economics just as in chess, success can often be put down to intuition and effective judgement [Simon, 1983]. Gary Kasparov, the famous Russian grand-master, maintained that

> Looking at every single possibility is a luxury we can't afford even in the limited realm of the chessboard [...] Looking ahead just a few moves can lead to hundreds of thousands of possible positions,

each the result of a cause and effect chain that has to be examined carefully. With so many possibilities expanding so quickly [. . .] the decision tree of 'if this then that, if that then this' has to be aggressively pruned [. . .]. Emotion and instinct cloud our strategic vision when there is no time for proper evaluation. Even the most honed intuition can't entirely do without accurate calculations. A game of chess can suddenly seem a lot like a game of chance. [Kasparov, 2007, pp. 46–159]

Whether we are talking about a business, a biological species or whatever, adaptation to the environment always depends, according to Simon, on a heuristic research and forms of local optimization or *satisficing* [Simon, 1984]. The search for alternatives ends with the one which, according to the circumstances, best satisfies our goals and needs. In this sense a theory of bounded rationality must first and foremost contemplate a theory of search [March, 1994] which does not conform to the normative rule for when to stop – the search for alternatives ending only when an optimal result is reached – but concentrates on personal levels of aspiration [Simon, 1957].

There are many kinds of aspiration: one may aspire to have an enjoyable job, to being in love, to good food or to travel the world. In each dimension the "expectation" of what one might obtain determines a level of aspiration that is matched against the actual experience. "Satisfaction" is achieved if the experience exceeds the level of aspiration one; "dissatisfaction" if the level of aspiration is not met [Simon, 1983]. If the processing of information matches or exceeds the initial level of aspiration, then the agent pursues the corresponding course of action because its is considered satisfying [Nozick, 1993]. On the contrary, dissatisfaction will lead to a lowering of the level of aspiration, followed by reconsidering an option that had previously been rejected or resumption of the search. In *organization theory* Simon points out that the study of levels of aspiration can make a substantial contribution to the enquiry into the two crucial topics of socio-organizational analysis: learning and innovation, processes which are based on the search for information and the accumulation of subjective experiences [Simon, 1957]. In this sense, while learning relates to the cognitive sphere of decision makers, the environment in which they operate and their abilities to elaborate and carry out specific programmes, innovation concerns the decisions of agents in favour of one option or another. But how will decision makers react in the face of either failures (pursuit of choice) or difficulty in representing the situation (hypothetical reasoning), or both of these together? Will they lower their aspirations and make do with satisfactory alternatives or react with a new search impulse? Simon argues that while it is undoubtedly true that successes lead to satisfaction and inertia, they nonetheless raise the expected value of the reward and hence the subsequent levels of aspiration, extending the search still further. Hence the close link between learning and innovation involves the role played by the level of aspiration. In Simon's model an innovation is preceded by a search and a learning experience which depend on the level of aspiration. Simon emphasises the importance of identifying the moment when innovation first begins in the context of an organization, especially when there is a change for the worse in environmental conditions that threatens the results achieved to date. Two types of adverse conditions spring to mind: a dip in the economic cycle, whether in progress or foreseen; and innovations introduced by competitors which improve their position in the market (Simon, 1958).

The process generally features the following sequences:

- if the change in the level of aspiration makes the state of the current decision unsatisfactory it can generate "searching";
- searching involves "learning";
- learning can lead to the adoption of an innovative option, meaning an option that was previously unknown but which is satisfactory with respect to the new level of aspiration.

Simon uses the metaphor of looking for the sharpest needle in a haystack to explain the concept of procedural rationality and satisfying choice. In fact, «most decisions are concerned not with searching for the sharpest needle in the haystack but with searching for a needle sharp enough to sew with» [*cited in* Pugh and Hickson, 2007, p. 190].

This procedural approach to rationality, less familiar than the concept of *bounded rationality*, shows the affinity between Simon and Hayek concerning knowledge. Like Hayek, Simon argued that human activity is not governed by an Olympian rationality (to use his own ironic definition) but by heuristic-adaptive processes that are successful in evolutionary terms because they set out to satisfy the organism's functional requisites. The procedural approach allows for the identification of at least three sources of endogenous change in the decision-making process:

- a cognitive representation of knowledge, which can vary from one decision maker to another and in the different phases of the decision-making process;
- a structuring of the objectives, which are not known a priori but are formulated during the decision-making process;
- criteria for pursuit of the search, the decision maker stopping at the

first satisfactory solution without pursuing an optimal solution [Simon, 1985].

Both Hayek's gnoseological fallibility and Simon's *bounded rationality* imply a radical revision of the neoclassical model of equilibrium. If in the neoclassical theory of economics the notion of rationality is closely connected to that of equilibrium, in the evolutionistic theory the notion of rationality goes hand in hand with disequilibrium. If optimal decisions – involving for example perfectly competitive markets – constitute the logical premiss of a general equilibrium, bounded rationality is associated with procedures of simplified calculation which require a different time span for each agent. Meanwhile new information can become available or be considered following the emergence of new conditions. Besides, it does not seem very likely that instances of human behaviour can be covered by a homeostatic scheme designed to reabsorb external tensions and achieve or reinstate optimal conditions. On the contrary, behaviour and psychological state, above all insofar as they are determined by goals and projects, tend to disrupt the pre-existing states of equilibrium and create dynamic evolutions; in other words they tend to disequilibrium, never to equilibrium or the tranquil vegetation of homeostasis [Israel, 2004, p. 139].

In this sense a decision is never a mere algorithmic elaboration of a set of data but an adaptive process which makes it possible to achieve a dynamic equilibrium between an effective, swift and economic decision, the progressive adjustments of the solution and, lastly, the final configuration of the reality following the problem's solution.

Although the idea that human behaviour does not follow logico-formal rules lies at the heart of *bounded rationality*, in view of the highly adaptive forms of reasoning which lie behind it, it cannot be considered irrational. As Selten has observed, it is possible to formulate theories of bounded rationality in which behaviour, although optimizing, is not irrational [Selten, 1998]. Simon set out to show the implausibility of an "abstract" rationality which ignores both external limits (*"task environment"*) and man's imperfect cognitive structure: factors which, in a representation of the decision-making process based on a scissors movement, constitute the two blades which conditon human rationality. Hence if in an absolute rational order the alternatives are given, in a bounded rational order they must be invented for each new situation by the agent, in a process that generates many possible actions [Simon, 1997]. The solution to environmental and computational problems is bound to be heuristic. It is interesting to note that Simon originally equated heuristics with *"rule of thumb"*, whereby agents proceed step by step. In order to avoid the types of conditioning we have mentioned, the agents arrive at the optimal choice by means of heuristic processes which, although potential causes of distortions (*biases*), are widely used to respond in a satisfactory manner to real problems.

In any case, *bounded rationality* cannot be invoked merely to explain human error: it invites us to reconsider the way information is represented. Just as the analysis of an enigmatic find enables an archaeologist to find out more about ancient civilizations, so the analysis of heuristics and biases carried out by Kahneman and Tversky, authentic "archaeologists of cognition" [Laibson and Zeckhauser, 1999], has provided important clues to the nature of human cognitive processes which have put paid to many of the misconceptions generated by the ideology of *homo œconomicus*.

Heuristics and Biases Approach

From the 1970s onwards the concept of heuristics took on experimental validity, constituting a significant challenge in the attempt to define a more realistic model of rational agent. In the research programme known as the *heuristics and biases approach* developed by Kahneman and Tversky, a series of decision-making problems were submitted to groups of individuals to discover whether they tackled them on the basis of rational criteria. This made it possible to investigate the limits of calculation and information processing which lead the individual to adopt highly adaptive heuristics. Heuristics is one of the most effective tools available to human rationality in order to reduce the cognitive load and arrive at rapid and generally effective responses to the problems [Hamilton and Gifford, 1976; Nisbett and Ross, 1980]. It is a strategy of non-reflective reasoning which enables individuals to choose compatibly with the complexity of the situation and the limits of their ability to store and process information, exploiting the inferential procedures sanctioned in the normative and probabilistic model. According to Kahneman, Slovic and Tversky [1982], heuristic judgement often constitutes the only practical way to evaluate uncertain elements. In fact, unlike what happens in formal calculus, heuristic evaluation of probability is generally based on immediate solutions which do not consider all the factors at stake, but only the peculiar features of the object being evaluated, the way in which the problem has been formulated, the clarity with which the situation has been described, and so on. These factors, whether separately or in conjunction, influence decision-making behaviour. Some principal types of heuristic reasoning have been identified – representativity, availability, anchoring and adjustment – with the affect heuristic as a more recent addition.

Representativity heuristic

The *representativity heuristic* is a cognitive strategy for estimating the probability or frequence of an event on the basis of resemblance [Nisbett and Ross, 1980] or *representativity*. For example, an individual is defined as representative by a certain social group on account of resemblance to typical features of the group, producing a very frequent type of *representativity* known as "category prediction".

One of the best known experiments carried out by Tversky and Kahneman [1983] to illustrate this heuristic was the so-called Linda problem. A group of participants were given a description of Linda's personality and a list of eight statements:

Linda is 31, single, outspoken and very bright. She graduated in philosophy. As a student, she was deeply concerned with issues of discrimination and social justice and also participated in anti-nuclear demonstrations.

- Linda is a psychiatric social worker
- Linda is a bank teller
- Linda is a teacher in a primary school
- Linda works in a bookshop and goes to yoga classes
- Linda is a member of Women Against Rape
- Linda is an active feminist
- Linda is a bank teller and an active feminist
- Linda is an insurance salesperson

The participants were divided into two groups. The first group were asked to order the eight statements according to their probability, and the second group according to their representativity, meaning how far Linda matches up to a typical member of that category. Most participants (89%) believed the statement «Linda is a bank teller and an active feminist » to be more probable than «Linda is a bank teller». Although there are circumstances in which the representativity heuristic leads to a correct judgement, the tendency to omit careful consideration of the underlying probabilities leads to what is known as *"base-rate neglect"*. The outstanding evolutionist Gould had this to say about the experiment:

I am particularly fond of [the Linda] example, because I know that the [conjunction] is least probable, yet a little homunculus in my head continues to jump up and down, shouting at me, "but she can't just be a bank teller: read the description.". . . Why do we consistently make this simple logical error? Tversky and Kahneman argue, correctly I think, that our minds are not built [for whatever reason] to work by the rules of probability. [1992, p. 469]

In other words, as in the Linda problem, he violates one of the fundamental tenets of probability theory: the principle of extendability. Specific results cannot be more probable than a more inclusive result. The consequence is a typical error of judgement known as the *conjunction fallacy*, whereby individuals wrongly attribute greater probabilities to composite events than to the single component events [Slovic, Fischhoff and Lichtenstein, 1976].

Availability heuristic

The *availability heuristic* is a cognitive strategy which involves evaluating the frequency or probability of an event on the basis of the facility with which this event can be called to mind and features in the memory. Ease of retrieval is considered indicative of the frequency of the object or the related event [MacLeod and Campbell, 1992]. In fact, when someone does not have precise data available they are likely to refer to previous knowledge, searching through their memory for elements which can be of help. The *availability* of such elements in the memory will make it easier for examples of the object or associations linked with it to be retrieved [Kahneman and Tversky, 1973]. In general, this criterion has an intrinsic validity in the sense that the data often confirm the intuitive judgement. However, this is not always the case. In a well-known experiment [Tversky and Kahneman, 1982] a text was devised, written in English, in which five consonants (k, l, n, r, v) appeared with a specific frequency in the first and third position in words of three or more letters. After having it read out, participants were asked to estimate the probability of these consonants appearing in the first or third position. Out of 152, 105 participants considered the first position to be more likely for most of the letters, as against 47 for the third: the latter was in fact the right answer. Kahneman and Tversky attributed the distortion to the *availability heuristic*: it is in fact easier to remember words which begin with a certain letter rather than words in which it appears in the third position.

More recent empirical research [Schwarz and Vaughn, 2002] has confirmed Tversky and Kahneman's hypothesis whereby the *availability heuristic* is grounded in the subjective impression of ease of retrieval and not the number of examples retrieved or generated. However, the process of memorisation draws on revision mechanisms of the stimuli which modify some fundamental aspects of the reality referred to. These processes can easily lead to distortions of judgement or biases. Among others, particular attention has been paid to the phenomenon of illusory correlation which occurs whenever a subject believes it is possible to identify a regular pattern in the conjunction of two entirely independent events. For example, when thinking of a certain type of event another quite different one may come to mind, leading us to infer that the two events are correlated. These fallacious hypotheses are borne out by mechanisms of selective attention that tend to identify a causality in the occurrence of events [Hamilton and Gifford, 1976].

Anchoring and adjustment heuristic

When asked to give an evaluation of an unknown event we often "anchor" our judgement to a known event:, perhaps a familiar element or one deriving from an authoritative or expert source. This phenomenon of "anchoring" is followed by a phase of adjustment, in which all the available information is analysed and integrated. Kahneman and Tversky [1973] showed that such phenomena represent one of the prime causes of error in the evaluation of probabilities, leading to systematic biases in the estimation of the factors of probability calculus. Recently Kahneman and others have set the heuristics and biases programme in the context of dual process theories. The key idea is that, in expressing a judgement or a decision, people can resort to two different cognitive systems: intuitive processes (system 1) and analytic processes (system 2) [Kahneman and Frederick, 2002; Stanovich, 1999]. System 1 is primitive, rapid and associative; system 2 is slow, serial and deductive. System 1 produces a rapid response which can be subsequently approved, corrected or substituted by system 2 [even though as a rule this does not happen]. In the process of understanding messages the attributes which are highly accessible to system 1 (such as similarity, availability, fondness) become heuristic attributes for the final judgement. In other words, intuitive judgement occurs if a highly accessible attribute is used (elaborated by perception or by system 1), and if the control exercised by system 2 fails to intervene. Thus the process of attribute substitution is at the heart of a new conception of heuristics: an objective attribute (the probability or plausibility of an event) is replaced by a heuristic attribute which is more accessible to the mind (resemblance, availability, imaginability). Both representativity and availability heuristics conform to this new conception. The former presupposes the substitution of an objective attribute with an impression given by resemblance; the latter functions in the same way with availability or imaginability. On the contrary, the *anchoring and adjustment heuristic* is not grounded in the process of attribute substitution, and for this reason it is no longer considered a form of heuristics. In fact if the original definition of bias referred to an error caused by the use of a heuristic to evaluate an objective attribute in a context in which the use of such a heuristic is not justified [Bonini and Hadjichristidis, 2009], the new conception states that *bias* occurs not only because system 1 proposes a wrong answer but also because system 2 does not correct this answer.

LET US CONSIDER THE FOLLOWING PROBLEM:

A pair of football boots and a ball together cost 110 euro; the boots cost 100 euro more than the ball; how much does the ball cost?

The most accessible answer, suggested intuitively by system 1, is 10 euro because the figure 110 euro is naturally broken down into 100 and 10. The right answer, however, is 5 euro. If the ball cost 10 euro, the pair of boots, which must cost 100 euro more, would cost 110 euro, meaning that boots and ball together come to 120 euro (110 euro for the boots and 10 for the ball). If, however, the ball costs 5 euro, the boots will cost 105 euro, coming to the correct total for boots and ball of 110 euro. According to Kahneman and Frederick [2005], the error occurs because system 2 has not controlled and corrected the intuitive response of system 1.

Affect heuristic

Sometimes people believe they are choosing on the basis of purely rational considerations, but, as Zajonc [1980] put it: «We do not just see 'a house': we see a handsome house, an ugly house, or a pretentious house"» [p. 154]. In most cases, in fact, we choose the option we like best, and only subsequently do we put forward rational justifications.

The *affect heuristic* shows how people do not decide in emotively neutral conditions but rather on the basis of an assessment of events and/or objects combined with an affective bias which influences their final judgement. Various empirical studies have shown the existence of a strong link between images, affectivity and decisions. Some have used the technique of word association: participants are confronted with verbal stimuli, usually one word or a very short phrase, and asked to name the first thought or image that comes to mind. Subsequently they are asked to assign to each response an "affective" score on a scale ranging from "very negative" (e.g. – 2) to "very positive" (e.g. + 2). It is then possible to calculate for each stimulus an affective index used to label each stimulus. Slovic and his research group [1991] used this method to measure the affective meanings people attribute to various cities and states [for example San Diego, Denver etc.], showing how the affective label for each stimulus (such as a holiday destination, for example) influenced their choices. The emotions experienced depend on the type of representation that comes to mind when we are stimulated by a word or event. This phenomenon, known as the *focusing illusion*, shows how people concentrate on some representations and not on others [Savadori and Rumiati, 2005]. For example, we generally associate positive images with the word "summer", even though in our memory we undoubtedly also store negative images such as the hardships caused by drought.

These instances of focusing guide our choices in all sorts of familiar situations. Recent studies have shown how an affective evaluation can guide our investments on the stock exchange [MacGregor *et al.*, 2000]. The emotions represent an important system of monitoring for relations between the individual and the environment because they pinpoint situations that regard us directly, highlighting what is at stake and which resources we can call on in order to modify these situations. In this sense they fulfill both a communicative and a motivational function. In the former the subject is rapidly alerted to the situation with respect to his/her needs and goals, showing third parties, by means of non verbal language, the affective reaction in progress; the latter consists in preparing the organism to react to the emotive situation, adopting appropriate modes of behaviour, which may involve inaction or the rejection of inter-relations, as when somebody is feeling demoralised.

Some authors have postulated the existence of authentic decision-making styles which define modalities of individual reaction within certain contexts. Now, if it is true that there are decision-making styles which individuals adopt more frequently than others, it is equally true that these styles are not rigid or immutable [Glaser and Weber, 2005], but rather flexible and modifiable in response to specific situations [Driver, Brousseau and Hunsaker, 1990]. Numerous decision-making styles have been identified and described. The simplest refer to a sort of bi-polarity corresponding to specific decision-making modalities. An example is the deliberative-intuitive dimension [Epstein *et al.*, 1996] which distinguishes between individuals who decide in an analytical and reflexive manner and those who decide rapidly and intuitively. Other, more complex typologies of decision-making styles describe multiple dimensions.

Scott and Bruce [1995] identified five decision-making styles:

- rational: characterized by a complete search for information, consideration of the possible alternatives and evaluation of their consequences;
- intuitive: based on attention to global aspects rather than systematic processing of information, and on the tendency to decide on the basis of intuition and feelings;
- dependent: typical of people who prefer to receive suggestions before making any choice at all;

- evasive: typical of individuals who tend to put off or avoid decisions;
- spontaneous: characterised by the propensity to decide as quickly as possible.

To measure these decision-making styles Scott and Bruce developed the General Decision Making Style (GDMS) inventory for defining individual decisional profiles. A different approach to distinguishing between modes of decision making was proposed by Schwarz and his group [2002]. Instead of identifying a specific decision-making style, this focuses on the tendency to look for the best possible result (the "optimizer") or to settle for a sufficiently good alternative (the "satisficer"). They developed a Maximization Scale distinguishing between people who tend to base their decisions on comparison with others, and then show themselves dissatisfied with the choice made, and those who by settling for an option which is "good enough" but not necessarily the best, register a fair level of satisfaction with respect to their decision. More than a century ago William James outlined a profile of the decision-making types.

> The first may be called the reasonable type. It is that of those cases in which the arguments for and against a given course seem gradually and almost insensibly to settle themselves in the mind and to end by leaving a clear balance in favor of one alternative, which alternative we then adopt without effort or constraint [. . .]. A "reasonable" character is one who has a store of stable and worthy ends, and who does not decide about an action till he has calmly ascertained whether it be ministerial or detrimental to any one of these [. . .]. In the second type of case our feeling is to a certain extent that of letting ourselves drift with a certain indifferent acquiescence in a direction accidentally determined from without, with the conviction that, after all, we might as well stand by this course as by the other, and that things are in any event sure to turn out sufficiently right. In the third type the determination seems equally accidental, it comes from within, and not from without [. . .]. There is a fourth form of decision, which often ends deliberation as suddenly as the third form does. It comes when, in consequence of some outer experience or some inexplicable inward change, we suddenly pass from the easy and careless to the sober and strenuous mood, or possibly the other way [. . .]. All those "changes of heart", "awakenings of conscience", etc., which make new men of so many of us, may be classed under this head [. . .]. In the fifth and final type of decision, the feeling that the evidence is all in, and that reason has balanced the books, may be either present or absent. But

in either case we feel, in deciding, as if we ourselves by our own wilful act inclined the beam: in the former case by adding our living effort to the weight of the logical reason which, taken alone, seems powerless to make the act discharge; in the latter by a kind of creative contribution of something instead of a reason which does a reason's work. [James 1950, pp. 796–798]

Prospect Theory and the Framing Effect

Prospect theory was one of the first theories to be elaborated as an alternative to expected utility. It was presented by Kahneman and Tversky in 1979 in the journal Econometrica, in an article entitled *Prospect Theory: An Analysis of Decision under Risk*. With its innovative approach, experimental soundness and the interpretation of the behavioural data that emerged from the experiments, the article made a major contribution to changing the general view of rationality and maximisation as presented in the neoclassical model. The authors argued that in interpreting and evaluating the proposed options or prospects individuals deviate from the status quo. According to this theory, the decision-making process has two phases. In the first phase the decision maker analyses the problem according to six different modalities:

- Formulation in terms of gain or loss according to the chosen standpoint;
- Segregation or isolation of the components presenting no risk;
- Cancellation of elements which are common to the various alternatives;
- Combination of analogous outcomes;
- Simplification in terms of rounding probabilities up or down;
- Ascertainment of dominance, meaning which alternatives prevail over the others, cancelling out the latter.

In the second phase the agent compares the various prospects and chooses the one of highest value. *Prospect theory* differs from the theory of expected utility on account of at least three important aspects: 1] the concept of value replaces that of utility; 2] utility is defined in terms of the greatest realizable gain/profit/earning; 3] value is defined in terms of gains or losses, or in other words of increments with respect to a neutral reference point.

As can be seen at S on the curve [Figure 4], by replacing the concept of utility with that of value agents reveal different attitudes to gains and losses (the function is convex for losses and concave for gains). In fact,

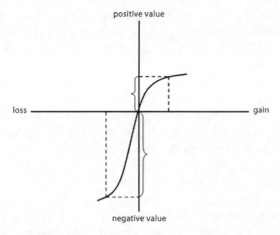

Figure 4 Prospect Theory

they attribute a very negative value to losses (the more one loses the more desperate one becomes), while high gains carry a positive value, but the satisfaction diminishes as the gains increase. Furthermore, in the domain of losses the utility function slopes more steeply than in that of gains, confirming the principle of *loss aversion* [Kahneman and Tversky, 1979] whereby – the final result being equal – the suffering caused by losses is greater than the pleasure caused by gains. This type of mental accounting violates the postulates of neoclassical economic theory and exerts a considerable influence on our decisions [Shefrin and Thaler, 1992]. For example, in a lottery the regret over marginal losses easily surpasses the happiness deriving from comparable gains, a situation that contradicts the implications of the maximisation of expected utility. The second difference concerns the way of viewing the probabilities associated with the outcomes. While the expected utility theory assumes that the decision maker evaluates a 50% probability of winning a given sum as meaning that there is a 50% likelihood of him winning, *prospect theory* introduces a function of deliberation which transforms the probabilities into "decision weighting" (a subjective assessment of the different options available) which is often subject to distortions with respect to the actual probabilities. In particular individuals tend to underestimate the low probabilities and overestimate the medium or high probabilities.

Moreover *prospect theory* maintains that the preferences depend on how the problem is envisaged, in the so-called *framing effect*. The decision maker may come to two antithetical decisions depending on his/her conception of the problem, or indeed on how it is presented, quite possibly with intent to influence the choice. Thus it is that we prefer a yoghurt comprising 95% of non-fat material to one with 5% fat, or a pullover which is advertised as 80% pure cashmere rather than 20% wool mix. According to Tversky and Kahneman [1981], alternative descriptions of the same problem can give rise to different preferences. In the first phase the agent *frames* the available choices, the possible outcomes and the respective probabilities in relation to the options adopted. The second phase – involving assessment and hence making the choice – is determined by the individual perception of the decision-making context and the impact of the decision's format. In fact in the assessment process the requisites of coherence for rational behaviour are not fully met. The *frames* induce individuals to use the information in the form suggested by the stimulus [Slovic, 1972], paying attention to only certain aspects of the alternatives, making a false estimate of the consequences and, lastly, examining only part of the information available. Thus rather than being appraised in absolute terms, the value of an alternative is assessed in relation to the context. Losses or gains, for example, have a different cognitive impact on the agent since they affect the importance of the information available and influence the propension to risk [Tversky, Sattah and Slovic, 1988].

A classic experiment proposed by Kahneman and Tversky [1984], known as the problem of the "Asian disease", shows clearly that the simple alternative "lives saved" and "lives lost" reverses the preferences of the agent and a sentiment of aversion gives way to behaviour involving risk. A group of individuals were informed of the imminence of an epidemic which would cause the death of 600 people. Two options were available for dealing with the situation, A or B in a first experiment and C or D in a subsequent one [Figure 5]:

THUS BY
- adopting plan A, 200 people will be saved;
- adopting plan B, there is 1/3 of chances that 600 people will be saved and 2/3 that no one will be saved.

Most respondents preferred plan A (the certain option). Another group of individuals were asked to choose between the two plans formulated differently:

- adopting plan C, 400 people will die;
- adopting plan D, there is 1/3 of chances that no one dies and 2/3 that 600 people die.

In this case most respondents preferred plan D (the option involving risk). Alternatives A and C, as indeed B and D, actualy produce identical

Experiment 1 (N: 252)	choice	Experiment 2 (N: 155)	choice
A 200 people will be saved	72%	C 0 people will die	22%
B 1/3 of chances that 600 people will be saved 2/3 of chances that no one will be saved	28%	D 1/3 of chances that 0 people will die 2/3 of chances that 600 people will die	78%

Figure 5 Problem of the Asian Disease

results. However, when the problem is formulated in terms of loss (lives lost) the goal becomes the reduction of the number of victims to zero, even though, on account of people's reluctance to submit to the risk involved, the chances of success are quite low. On the other hand, when formulated in terms of gain (lives saved) the goal becomes making that gain as certain as possible, foregoing results which would be better but are less probable (risk aversion).

An interesting extension of *prospect theory* concerns the so-called theory of *mental accounting* formulated by Thaler [1999]. His research into the way problems are reformulated showed that in most cases people operate according to the principle of *concreteness* [Slovic, 1972], whereby the initial message we receive determines the way in which we interpret the information and the types of connection we make between one factor and another. In other words, the decision maker only deals with the information (for example, gains and losses) explicitly indicated in the stimulus received, and uses it in exactly the form in which it was presented. Thaler [1980] introduced the term *mental accounting* to indicate the ways in which individuals gather and catalogue information. His theory – applied to decisions which imply comparisons between multiple attributes and dimensions, like those concerning consumer goods – posits that economic choices are mediated by an authentic system of "mental accounting" which is not neutral; nor does it conform to the postulates of normative rationality, but exerts a significant influence on choice.

Mental accounting has three fundamental characteristics: 1] it forms an idea of the extent of costs and benefits before and after the choice; 2] people classify activities on the basis of a certain value; 3] it is a dynamic process, flexible over time and dependent on the contingency connected with decision making in situations of uncertainty [Thaler, 1999]. Using the premises of *prospect theory* , Thaler was able to explain two anomalies not contemplated by *rational choice* in economics: the *sunk cost effect* and the *endowment effect*. The former concerns the tendency of individuals to choose on the basis of previous decisions, taking into account costs already sustained [*sunk cost*], rather than of evaluations of the future consequences, as is the case in normative models. Arkes and Blumer [1985] showed that individuals decide differently according to whether they are informed or not of the costs already sustained and that cannot be recuperated. For example, if people are told that a certain capital sum has been invested in a project, the tendency will be to complete the investment even knowing that it will lead to losses and that the capital will not be recouped. On the contrary, if they are not aware of money invested previously, they will decide to abandon the project. This second phenomenon refers to the tendency to think that objects in one's possession (*endowment*) are worth more than the value they had when they were acquired.

The *endowment effect* generates an authentic "status quo bias" [Kahneman, Knetsch and Thaler, 1991], determined by the heuristic principle of *loss aversion*. It follows that the maximum sum people are willing to pay to acquire a certain good is lower than the minimum sum they are willing to accept when selling. Losses are rated more highly than gains; furthermore people are unwilling to relinquish an object simply by virtue of the fact that it is theirs [Thaler, 1980]. This difference is completely ignored by neoclassical economic theory. *Mental accounting* posits that this effect arises because the economic agents do their utmost to avoid wasting money by paying for goods they then do not use, because this results in *loss aversion* and thus a marked diminution in utility. The local organization of *mental accounting* induces people to evaluate gains and losses in relative rather than absolute terms, and this explains the great variations in people's willingness to buy according to the situation in which they find themselves.

Let us consider two problems which show the effect of local *mental accounting*. One is the so-called "theatre problem" [Tversky and Kahneman, 1981] in which participants are presented with two versions of the same scenario, structured respectively as "the loss of a ticket" and "the loss of a banknote":

- Problem 1 (N = 200): imagine you have decided to go and see a show and have already paid 50 euro for the ticket. On arriving at the theatre you find you have lost the ticket. Would you be willing to pay a further 50 euro to purchase another ticket?
  YES (46%) NO (54%)
- Problem 2 (N = 183): imagine you have decided to go and see a show costing 50 euro. On arriving at the theatre you find you have

lost a 50 euro banknote. Would you be willing to pay 50 euro anyway to see the show?
YES (88%) NO (12%)

It is clear that in both formulations the loss in monetary terms is exactly the same. However, as Tversky and Kahneman [1981] point out, a different mental representation of the two events induces the individuals to attribute a different "value" to losing 50 euro. In the first situation they appear to add the cost of the second ticket to the cost of the one they lost, making a total cost of 100 euro which is considered excessive. In the second case most of the participants do not associate the loss of 50 euro with the purchase of the ticket but mentally debit the sum lost to a "separate account".

Empirical and theoretical research developed in connection with the psychology of decision making suggests that cognitive strategies follow paths that are frequently differ from those postulated by rational choice. According to the model of the adaptive decision maker developed by Payne, Bettman and Johnson [1993], the decision-making process is a highly contingent form of information processing whereby individuals use adaptive decision-making strategies and heuristics in response to both their limited capacity for processing information and the complexity of the tasks. A decision-making strategy is a sequence of conative and cognitive mental operations [acting on the environment] which transform the state of initial knowledge into final knowledge that can be brought to bear on the problem in question. Cognitive strategies are selected in relation to a series of factors: the way in which the information is presented, the complexity of the problem, the decision-making context and the characteristics of the decision maker [Hastie and Dawes, 2001]. Such variables, regardless of the values of the alternatives, influence the selection of the strategies by modifying the cognitive effort necessary for implementing them [Bettman, 1993].

Everyday experience shows that, when faced with various situations, we make decisions in a non-stereotypical way. A fundamental characteristic of our cognitive system is in fact the extraordinary flexibility of the decision-making strategies at our disposal. First of all, when "deciding how to decide", individuals consider accuracy and cognitive effort not as absolute attributes connected to a strategy, but rather as properties dependent on a specific situation. Such an assessment – established either beforehand (top-down) or during the accomplishment of the task [bottom-up] and the processing of the decision itself – can influence the choice of the various decision-making strategies at one's disposal. The strategy chosen will be the one that allows the decision maker to come to a good decision with the least possible effort. The most frequent simplification strategies [Payne, Bettman and Johnson, 1993] are commonly classified as compensatory and non compensatory. Compensatory strategies require a quantitative judgement and are applied when the options or the attributes which describe the various alternatives are commensurable on the basis of their attractiveness/utility values. In other words, an individual chooses the alternative having an attribute that compensates for the sacrifice he/she is willing to make by renouncing consideration of other attributes.

Non compensatory strategies, instead, are used for those decision-making problems in which options and criteria are incommensurable and the limited attractiveness of an option in relation to a certain criterion cannot be compensated by the greater attractiveness of the same option in relation to another criterion. Individuals often have to mediate between accuracy and effort in the selection of a strategy according to the requirements of the task: in such cases a certain flexibility is necessary in the strategies to be adopted. The decision-making process, considered as a limited capacity cognitive activity, in fact aims at satisfying several objectives, such as minimising emotional strain due to the presence of conflictual values among alternatives [Hogarth, 1987], reaching socially acceptable and justifiable decisions, and making accurate decisions which maximise advantages and minimise the cognitive effort required for acquiring and processing information [Simon, 1978]. Minimising cognitive effort is defined on the basis of the amount of time and the type of mental operation required for putting a certain decision-making strategy into action. Zipf [1949] proposes the principal of minimal cognitive effort, according to which a strategy is chosen that ensures the minimum effort in the reaching of a specific desired result. The strategies that involve more accurate choices are often those that entail more effort. Hence the choice of strategies is the result of a compromise between the desire to make the most correct decision and the desire to use the smallest amount of effort [Johnson and Payne, 1985]. The following list describes some compensatory and non compensatory strategies reported in the literature:

Compensatory strategies

- Additive Difference (ADD): this is based on the comparison between two options at a time, attribute by attribute. The differences between the attributes are added up for an overall comparison between the two options. The best alternative is then compared with the next option and so on. The chosen option is the one that comes out top in all the comparisons [Tversky, 1969].
- Equal Weights (EQW): this examines all of the alternatives and

values attributed to each alternative, ignoring the information relative to the importance or the probability of each attribute [Dawes,1979]. In other words, the option having the highest score in terms of general utility is chosen. General utility is defined as the sum of the utilities of each option.

- The Multi-Attribute Utility Model (MAU): this is a normative rule which causes the choice to fall on the option with the greatest utility. The greatest utility is defined as the sum of the utilities of the various attributes [Anderson, 1974].

- The Majority of Confirming Dimensions (MCD): this includes, as in the ADD strategy, the examination of pairs of options. The values of each of the two options are compared on the basis of each attribute. The option with the largest quantity of winning attributes is kept and compared with the next option. The comparison in pairs comes to a halt when all of the options have been evaluated and the final winning option has been identified [Russo and Dosher, 1983].

Non compensatory strategies

- Disjunctive (DIS): in this strategy a product is assessed in relation to its best characteristic while disregarding the others. For example, when purchasing a vehicle I may decide to purchase a model that has excellent performance in terms of cost without worrying about its performance in relation to other factors.

- Elimination-By-Aspects (EBA): this is based on the idea that a decision maker does not evaluate the alternatives as such, but rather on the basis of their characteristics. The decision maker selects one aspect and eliminates from the alternatives all those which do not include that particular aspect. For example, in the case of a vehicle, one aspect could be whether or not the car has an airbag. In the case of on-going aspects [such as the price or the additional costs of the vehicle] the decision maker establishes minimum levels and eliminates all of the alternatives below those levels. The process of elimination continues until only one option remains [Tversky 1972].

- Lexicographic (LEX): this consists of evaluating the available options solely on the basis of the most important characteristic, choosing the option that shows the best value for that characteristic. In the case of options which have the same value in relation to the most important characteristic, the best options are evaluated with regard to the next characteristic in order of importance and so on [Fishburn 1974].

- Recognition Heuristic (REC): in some choices, people have so little information that they simply choose the first alternative familiar to them. In many cases, the recognition heuristic works well. This can be considered as a particular case of the LEX strategy, with the difference that in this case the most important attribute is the recognition of the object's name. If there are several options with the same value, the option with the best value for the second most important attribute is chosen and so on [Goldstein and Gigerenzer 2002].
- Satisficing (SAT)/Conjunctive Heuristic: the decision maker considers only one alternative at a time and compares the value of each one of its attributes with a predefined value threshold or aspiration level. The alternative is chosen or rejected according to whether all of its attributes have values above or below the threshold in question. The choice will fall on the most satisfactory alternative in relation to all of the attributes considered, namely the alternative that satisfies the pre-established minimum standards. The conjunctive rule is clearly of the "satisficing" type: for an alternative to be selected, all it has to do is satisfy the pre-established standards (or aspiration levels) for all of the attributes considered.
- Random: the choice is made without consulting any of the available information. Such a strategy can be used when time is at a premium or in the case of a highly complex task. In general, individuals can adapt, substitute or combine decision-making strategies thanks to their flexible use. In the case of a recombination of the strategies there is an initial phase in which the weakest alternatives are eliminated and a second phase in which the remaining alternatives are examined in greater detail [Payne 1976].

Decision-making strategies are clearly not circumscribed by a logical structure. In the majority of concrete situations an optimal assessment of the alternatives would be computationally unsustainable, influenced by prejudices, fatigue, time, limited information and other factors. The performance of natural logic has acted, as it were, as the "invisible hand" in the evolution of the human race. Nonetheless, from Aristotle to Frege the attempt to identify the logical laws subtending our abilities to think and reason has progressively shifted in focus from natural language – in which it sought to detect the underlying logical structures – to a purely formal language which is in many ways inadequate for describing the actual functioning of human thought.

HEURISTICS, BIASES AND ECOLOGICAL DECISION MAKING

Decisions in Conditions of Risk and Uncertainty

During the 20th century economists and mathematicians went to great lengths to neutralise risk and associated concepts such as uncertainty and unforeseeability. The demonstration of the limits of the neoclassical paradigm based on the simple calculation of costs and benefits made it more difficult to arrive at a scientific evaluation of risk and uncertainty. From the seventies onwards a large quantity of theoretical and empirical studies have investigated the heuristic principles and cognitive strategies which individuals use to deal with risky and uncertain situations. This research has shown how the explicative and predictive shortcomings of normative risk analysis depend in many respects on undervaluing the continuous interaction between the individual and the environment. These are factors which day by day represent significant obstacles in decision making [Brunsson, 1985; Thompson, 1967]. Conventionally, when one speaks of uncertainty one refers to situations in which the individual knows the outcomes of the choice but not the probabilities involved. The problem of uncertainty is central to the study of decision-making processes because the consequences of the actions an individual undertakes are often prolonged into the future, and one can never be completely sure that the hoped-for outcome will in fact be achieved. Although uncertainty is a key concept in discussions of decision making, there is no real consensus of opinion as to its meaning. One can find as many definitions of it as there are ways of approaching it [Argote, 1982; Yates and Stone, 1992]. The table [Figure 6] gives a good illustration of the proliferation of definitions of uncertainty and associated terms (for

AUTHORS	TERM	CONCEPTUALIZATION
I. Behavioral Decision Theory		
1. Anderson *et al.* (1981)	Uncertainty	A situation in which one has no knowledge about which of several states of nature has occurred or will occur.
2. Anderson *et al.* (1981)	Uncertainty	A situation in which one knows only the probability of which of several possible states of nature has occurred or will occur.
3. Humphreys & Berkeley (1985)	Uncertainty	The inability to assert with certainty one or more of the following: a) act-event sequences; b) event-event sequences; c) value of consequences; d) appropriate decision process; e) future preferences and actions; f) one's ability to affect future events.
4. Anderson *et al.* (1981)	Risk	Same as (1)
5. Anderson *et al.* (1981)	Risk	Same as (2)
6. MacCrimmon & Wehrung (1986)	Risk	Exposure to the chance of loss in a choice situation.
7. Arrow (1965)	Risk	A positive function of the variance of the probability distribution of expected positive and negative outcomes.
8. Hogart (1987)	Ambiguity	Lacking precise knowledge about the likelihood of events (second-order probability).
II. Organizational Decision Theory		
9. Thompson	Task Uncertainty	The inability to act deterministically owing to lack of cause-effect understanding: environmental dependencies and internal interdependencies.
10. Galbraith (1973)	Task Uncertainty	The difference in the amount of information required to perform a task and the amount of information already possessed by the organization.
11. March & Olsen (1976)	Ambiguity	Opaqueness in organizations owing to inconsistent or ill-defined goals; obscure causal relations in the environment unclear history, and interpersonal differences in focus attention.
12. Terreberry (1968)	Turbolence	Unpredictable changes in system-environment relations.
13. Weick (1979)	Equivocality	The multiplicity of meanings which can be imposed on a situation.
14. March & Simon (1958)	Conflict	Absence of arguments which clearly favor a particular course of action.

Figure 6 The Proliferation of Definitions of Uncertainty and Associated Terms

example, risk, ambiguity and equivocality) that can be found in 30 years of literature on decision making.

In order to clarify the nature of the uncertainty, Lipshitz and Strauss [1997] identified three basic situations:

- uncertainty is the sense of doubt that blocks or delays action. We can identify three essential features in this definition: 1) it is subjective (different people can be subject to different doubts in identical situations); 2) it is inclusive (no particular form of doubt, such as ignorance of future results, is specified); 3) it conceptualises uncertainty in terms of its effect on action (hesitation, indecision, procrastination);

- the uncertainty with which decision makers must cope depends on the model of decision making adopted. In other words, models implemented which have different informational requisites [Grandori, 1984] will be blocked or delayed by different doubts;

- different types of uncertainty can be classified according to their issue (what the decision maker is unsure about) and source (what determines the uncertainty). The fundamental problems include results, situations and alternatives. As for the causes, incomplete information is the most commonly cited cause of uncertainty [Galbraith, 1973; Smithson, 1989]. On occasions, however, decision makers are incapable of acting not so much out of lack of information but because they are disoriented by conflicts generated by the surfeit of meanings the information gives rise to [Weick, 1995]. Moreover the causes of uncertainty are not limited to incomplete information and inadequate comprehension. Decision makers may be prevented from acting even if they have understood the alternatives perfectly but are unable to differentiate between them.

The concept of uncertainty goes hand in hand with that of risk: a risky situation is always determined by a certain degree of uncertainty concerning the results of future actions. If the outcome of a course of action is guaranteed, risk is non-existent. The assessment of the degree of risk and uncertainty is one of the main components of every decision-making process. From the terms of insurance on the first transatlantic crossings to the development of the welfare state, the calculation of risks and efforts to make the contingencies foreseeable and manageable are part of the epic narratives of human history [Beck, 2003]. As we have said, there are many definitions of risk in the literature, some of them contradictory. While some, closely linked to the theory of probability, seek to give an objective definition – as the probability of loss – others favour a subjective and contextual investigation. From a conceptual standpoint it is important to distinguish between risk and danger, which are often treated as synonyms. If a danger has highly probable negative consequences and indicates a characteristic of the harmful object or situation [e.g. fire, electricity, virus, radiation, speed and so on], risk incorporates the danger, the probability of its occurrence and the potential seriousness of the damage [Yates and Stone, 1992]. Thus in general, risk indicates the probability that, using a certain instrument or implementing a certain behaviour, an individual will encounter danger [Lupton, 2003].

Risk analysis requires the following elements: a risk scenario (R), a range of consequences (D = damage) and a probability of the occurrence of the risk phenomenon (P) [Kaplan and Garrick, 1981]. These factors make it possible to formally define risk as the relation between the entity of a possible damage and the probability of the dangerous event occurring ($R = P \times D$). However, in many cases knowledge of such probabilities is not very exact, and may indeed be non-existent. In the latter case we are dealing with decisions in conditions of uncertainty or ignorance [Lopes, 1997].

The first attempt to define the concepts of uncertainty and risk were made by the economist Knight, who, in Risk, uncertainty and profit [1921] distinguished between measurable and non-measurable uncertainty, referring to the former as risk and the latter as uncertainty.

Uncertainty must be taken in a sense radically distinct from the familiar notion of Risk, from which it has never been properly separated. The essential fact is that "risk" means in some cases a quantity susceptible of measurement, while at other times it is something distinctly not of this character; and there are far-reaching and crucial differences in the bearings of the phenomena depending on which of the two are really present and operating. [Knight, 1921, pp. 19–20]

Starting from Knight's theories, economics has attempted, on one hand, to reduce uncertainty, and on the other to make the perception of risk objective by applying mathematical models to economic problems deriving from games theory and decision-making theory. According to Arrow [1951] and Lucas [1981] economics undoubtedly deals with risk but not with uncertainty. On his part, Keynes held that it is by no means enough for similar events to have happened in the past for them to recur. In a statement verging on paradox, the great British economist affirmed that our confidence in a hoped-for outcome can be reinforced only when we can find a situation in which a new series of events differs significantly from any encountered previously [Keynes, 1952].

Risk assessment became a topic of scientific enquiry in the last half century, as a result above all of public concern about the increasingly dangerous consequences of the use of nuclear energy. The first scientific study on the perception of risk was carried out by the director of the Atomic International Division, Starr. Published in *Science* in 1969, it looked at safety in nuclear power stations and proposed a procedure for calculating the level of technological risk acceptable to society in view of the attendant social benefits. Even though it relied on a mathematical/probabilistic evaluation of risk, the results revealed an enormous discrepancy between the objective risk and the perception on the part of the population. The variant of "social acceptance" soon proved to be complex, eluding concrete estimates and classifications, leading researchers to talk about different levels of risk. In particular, it was shown that the risks perceived as voluntary (such as risks associated with smoking or the failure to prevent certain illnesses) were considered more acceptable and less probable than the risks perceived as involuntary or imposed (as for example those of nuclear power stations). Moreover, as is shown by Starr's correlation function [1969] [Figure 7], when the events are very familiar, objective and perceived risk coincide; as they become less frequent, the perceived risk increases unduly; and finally, in cases of extreme rarity, it diminishes unduly [Starr and Whipple, 1980; Slovic, 2000].

Following Starr's research discussion of risk, which had been restricted

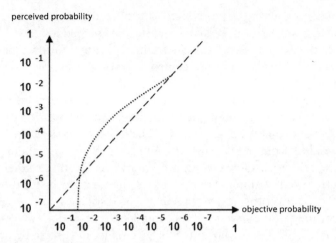

Figure 7 Starr's Correlation Function

to the sphere of technological safety, spread to such sectors as psychology and sociology. Psychology has contributed considerably to risk analysis, progressing from the classic concept of the calculation of probabilities of an undesirable event to the concept of subjective risk based on perception and individual evaluation. In this line of research the most commonly used methodology is known as the psychometric paradigm, proposed by Slovic and his group. The main aim of this research is to identify the mental strategies people use in formulating risk assessments [Di Nuovo, 2008]. These studies have shown how the perception of risk depends on various factors quite apart from the objective risk: degree of control, seriousness of the consequences, previous knowledge and experiences, perceived benefits and others [Slovic, 1987]. In everyday life, above all in situations which require specific, contingent evaluations or in situations where time is at a premium, risk perception is based above all on subjective, intuitive judgements and is thus often exposed to distortions or bias, of which the following are the most frequent.

Illusion of control

The illusion of control influences a lot of our day to day behaviour, such as driving at high speed or failure to use safety belts. It is a systematic tendency to believe you can control situations so as to influence the outcome, even if it is predominantly a matter of chance [Langer, 1975]. People tend to believe that the risks inherent in such behaviour can be controlled by their own ability. In reality, this betrays an excessive and unjustified belief in oneself (overconfidence), since even an expert driver cannot control all the factors which contribute to causing a road accident [Rumiati, 2000]. Research carried out into the perception of risk among Italian adolescents [Savadori and Rumiati, 1996] showed a clear link between the decisive nature of control and risk perception. Adolescents who regularly drink alcohol believe they can control the related risks, indeed they think they are less at risk than those who never drink. Another very common example is smoking. Among occasional smokers (less than one cigarette a day) only 15% believed that over the next 5 years they would become heavy smokers. In reality, 5 years on about 43% of them had done so, showing a significant over-estimation of their ability to control events. Among heavy smokers, on the other hand, about 32% believed that over the next 5 years they would still be smoking, and 68% thought they would have given up. In reality 5 years on 70% continued to smoke. Thus those who smoke believe they can control their behaviour more than is actually the case in real life.

Unrealistic optimism

Unrealistic optimism [Slovic, Fischhoff and Lichtenstein, 1980] is closely connected to the illusion of control. It represents the difference between what we consider risky for ourselves and what we consider risky for others. In the face of a specific risk we quite often consider others to be at much greater risk: for example, drivers consider themselves more proficient and less at risk than other drivers. It has to be said that the bias is not a personality trait like character-based optimism [Scheier and Carver, 1987] but an incongruous evaluation of the probabilities of falling victim to a negative event. Unrealistic optimism derives from two dynamics, one cognitive and the other motivational. The first consists in overestimating the number and efficacy of the precautions you yourself take with respect to those taken by others. In fact one's own behaviour is more readily accessible in one's memory than that of others. As a consequence, in assessing one's own degree of risk exposure, the evaluation is distorted by a recollection that favours oneself [Weinstein, 1980]. The second dynamic shows how the individual also uses optimistic distortions to safeguard self esteem. If there were no such distortions, in fact, we would perceive the risks inherent in consciously dangerous activities – such as smoking or driving without a seatbelt – and this would reflect badly on our self image. Numerous experiments have shown that this bias increases if the risky activities are considered to be controllable and we believe we are capable of controlling them effectively [Otten and Van Der Plight, 1996]. On the contrary, the bias diminishes or disappears altogether when we assess situations in which one cannot act to reduce the risk and when the group with whom one is comparing the personal risk is perceived as similar, close or affectively linked to oneself [Quadrel, Fischhoff and Doris, 1993]. Finally, in some conditions not only does the optimistic bias disappear but it is replaced by pessimistic bias [Dolinsky, Gromsky and Zawinsza, 1986], a tendency which is apparently correlated to the nature of the risk. If, in fact, the optimistic bias characterises risks which are incidental, potential and familiar, pessimistic bias corresponds to risks perceived as common, real and unfamiliar (for example the health effects linked to radiation following a nuclear accident). In terms of adaptation, in fact, in the first case an optimistic attitude can free us from anxiety and help us to cope more serenely with everyday activities; while in the second case one is induced to pay more attention to the risks and make more of an effort with preventive action [Norem and Cantor, 1986].

Expertise

Level of expertise generally influences risk evaluation, as numerous experiments go to show. In this context "experience" refers not to actual experiences of dangerous situations but to the competence of individuals (insurers, doctors, those responsible for risk technologies, and so on) acquired during their professional activity [Hendrickx and Vlek, 1991]. In the medical field, for example, the influence of the different level of experience has often been the subject of investigation in studies of the psychology of decision-making. Deciding in favour of one particular diagnosis or a specific therapy are paradigmatic examples of decision making in conditions of uncertainty and risk [Kuipers, Moskowitz and Kassirer, 1988] in which the reduction of the degree of uncertainty is closely correlated to the level of competence acquired [Patel and Groen, 1991]. Numerous studies have shown a superior performance among experts with respect to non experts in terms of the following factors:

- lower rate of errors recorded;
- better ability to formulate a correct diagnosis;
- better ability to correctly attribute the true diagnostic value to each specific symptom;
- rapid classification of the available information so as to formulate the diagnosis;
- tendency to be succinct in setting out the motives and reasons which led to the formulation of a specific diagnosis [Gilhooly, 1990].

Research carried out in this sector has shown that expert doctors are also better able to retrieve the knowledge acquired in the course of their training and professional activity [Ericsson, Patel and Kintsch, 2000]. In fact their mental structure for representing dominion specific knowledge is characterised not only by more available data but above all by a higher level of integration of the information acquired. Thus in evaluating the diagnosis which presents itself as a problem solving situation, the identification of symptoms – the value attributed to them and comparison with the full set of knowledge acquired – makes it possible to arrive at more correct and accurate inferences and diagnoses.

Confirmation bias

People often appear to base their judgement on information that confirms their hypotheses rather than the contrary. For example, in the classic selection task devised by Wason [1960], participants who were required to choose quickly tended to reproduce cases conforming to the rule they had hypothesised without considering cases that broke it. This occurs because among the strategies for selecting hypotheses there is often a tendency to verify only one type of forecast, which leads to inadequate hypotheses being confirmed. In interpreting events there is a tendency to attribute little importance to the contradictory information or else to only contemplate events which are coherent with one's expectations. In general the action of these tendencies in a certain sense makes the cognitive system conservative: selecting only positive information, giving little weight to contradictory information, reinforces one's own convictions rather than developing the habit of subjecting them to critical reappraisal.

Consent heuristic

Sometimes when we are uncertain as to what to do we observe others' behaviour to gather information which may help in our decisions. The others orient, more or less implicitly, our behaviour, alerting us to pitfalls or advantages. One of the first experimental studies of the phenomenon of conformism with respect to a majority was carried out by the psychologist Asch [1952]. In a classic experiment, he asked a group of participants to state whether two lines were the same length. All the participants were his accomplices apart from one. Asch discovered that it was enough for the other participants to answer in a certain way, even if it was patently wrong, for the judgement of the individual whose behaviour he was studying to be influenced. The result, borne out by much subsequent research, showed that when a reasonably large number of people reach a consensus on the assessment of an event, individuals taken one by one undergo a sort of psychological pressure and tend to adopt the common point of view in a reaction which is gregarious and conformist but rationally inexplicable. This heuristic strategy is adopted more commonly if the subject is unfamiliar or there is low motivation or limited possibility of processing the information (for example the subject does not interest us, or we are under stress). In the specific context of behaviours at risk (even if not in a work situation) it has been observed that, if we are given information on the preventive behaviour of others, this modifies our intentions concerning the use of safety measures in a directly proportional ratio. For example, if we know that only 12% in a group use safety measures, we will be less likely to use them ourselves than if that figure were 88% [Buunk, van den Eijnden and Siero, 2002].

Risk and Emotions

The impact of the emotions on risk assessment is well documented in the literature. Even though the emotions enable the individual to respond to all sorts of external events, the impulse to act associated with the various emotions persists beyond the current situation, affecting subsequent behaviour [Lerner and Keltner, 2000]. This impulse to act is well explained by the model of feelings as information [Schwarz, 1990], whereby the emotions act as a source of information with respect to the environment. Extending this line of research, Loewenstein and his collaborators [2001] showed that the choices made in situations of risk are in part the result of the direct influence of the emotive reactions on the cognitive process ("risk as feelings"). According to the authors, it is necessary to distinguish between anticipatory emotions, meaning the immediate, gut reactions experienced in situations of risk, and anticipated emotions, meaning the emotive reactions that the individual expects after taking a certain decision. Although both influence decisions in conditions of risk, the authors focused above all on the latter, showing how choices are often determined by what a person thinks they will feel after choosing one option rather than another. The study of regret [Bell, 1982; Looms and Sugden, 1982] constitutes a paradigmatic example of this phenomenon. An individual experiences regret on discovering that an alternative that had been discarded could have given better results. In fact a decision maker reckons not only in terms of gains but also of loss, setting the pleasure at what is acquired against the regret at what is missed. This theory introduces motivational and emotive factors into the study of decision-making behaviour. For when confronted with a decision, agents are usually led to avoid disagreeable emotive consequences and, at the same time, to pursue a positive emotion, avoiding regret at the choice made [Simonson, 1992]. The studies carried out by Loewenstein [2001] suggest that in conditions of risk, anticipatory emotions exert an influence on decisions. In fact emotive and rational reactions to situations of risk can diverge on account of risk assessment. Nonetheless judgement is often determined by the former rather than the latter. In a state of anger, for example, the tendency to impulsive behaviour and social or personal risk-taking tends to prevail [Harmon-Jones, 2003]. In an experimental study Lerner and Keltner [2000] demonstrated that angry people express more optimistic risk assessments and manifest risk-seeking behaviour. This conclusion is coherent with Lerner and Keltner's theory of assessment, whereby anger is associated with the perception of greater certainty and control over the outcome of one's behaviour and decisions.

On the contrary, sadness seems to be characterised by a lack of phys-iological excitation and thus scarce propensity to action, associated with a sense of resignation and impotence. This sensation reduces risk aver-sion, and the consequences of one's decisions are often attributed to the situation rather than to personal factors [DeSteno et al., 2000]. Fear and anxiety, while not being synonyms – fear in fact refers to knowable causes, while in anxiety the threat is represented by uncertainty regarding future states or situations concerning individual well-being – produce a common impulse concerning action: evasion or flight [Smith and Ellsworth, 1985]. In a state of anxiety there is no concrete threat prompting evasion or flight. The behavioural correlates of anxiety are more common, and the effects on behaviour more pervasive and long-lasting [Lazarus, 1991]. Fear and anxiety derive from assessments of uncertainty and lack of control over the situation. Unlike anger, they are associated with pessimistic evaluations of the environmental conditions. Thus people manifest a contrary impulse to action: instead of being opti-mistic with respect to risk, they display risk aversion and a pessimistic assessment of the situation [Lerner and Keltner, 2000]. A manager prone to fear or anxiety, for example, is likely to pay more attention to their own behaviour and arrive at a negative risk assessment [Fischhoff et al., 2005].

There is ample evidence to indicate that joy and happiness favour a sociable, cooperative attitude towards others, reducing interpersonal conflicts. Happiness induces a sense of security and control in people's perception of the environment, making them more ready to adopt risky decisions.

According to Lipshitz and Strauss [1997], in the descriptive or behav-ioural approach to the theory of decision making the standard methodology for facing up to uncertainties can be summarised in the acronym RQP: Reduce the uncertainty by means of a more thorough information search; Quantify the uncertainty that cannot be reduced; Plug the result into a formal scheme which includes the uncertainty as a factor in the choice of a specific course of action. They go on to say that the RQP heuristic is incomplete because it lacks the process of adoption of individual and environmental feedback found in most decision-making situations [Klein, 1998].

Naturalistic Decision Making

The recognition of these limits has fostered the conditions for a different approach to the study of decisions. Naturalistic Decision Making (NDM) sets out to study the way in which people make decisions and perform complex cognitive functions when dealing with real world problems: namely in situations characterized by time limits, incomplete knowledge of the alternatives, emotional tension, uncertainty, poorly defined objectives, high stakes and decision makers with various levels of experience. This study of decision making is not restricted to the mere choice among the available alternatives on the basis of their expected utility but covers the natural procedures followed by decision makers before carrying out an action. Such procedures follow three underlying principles:

1. the decisions are based on a holistic evaluation of the potential actions performed in the light of the available options as well as the comparison between the specific characteristics of those options [Lipshitz *et al.* 2001];
2. the decision maker chooses to act not on the basis of the search for and detailed processing of the alternatives, but through a process of situation recognition (the recognition-based heuristic) carried out by comparing the alternatives and the potential courses of action (pattern-matching) based on a handful of acceptability criteria;
3. rather than looking for an optimal solution, the decision maker adopts a satisficing choice criterion [Klein and Calderwood 1991].

Within the "naturalistic" approach to decision making we can identify three principal theories: Recognition-primed decision, Fast and frugal heuristics and Image theory.

Recognition-primed decision

The studies carried out by Klein and colleagues [1993] on decision making by experts (doctors, military commanders, fire fighters, pilots and others) have shown how in critical situations they tend not to follow normative models. When the decision-making process is subject to drastic time restrictions, there may be serious consequences if no decision or a wrong decision is taken. If, for example, a fire chief in an emergency situation does not decide what is to be done swiftly and effectively, he risks putting the lives of many people at risk. Often the objectives are not clear (is it necessary to bring people to safety or put out the fire quickly?), information is uncertain (he may not have a clear idea of the layout of the building or what material is stored there) and the intervention procedures are not always codified (perhaps a rescuer will have to use their imagination to find a way of freeing a trapped victim).

People who are expert in their sector decide by making a rapid review of the situations and experiences already encountered. In particular, they quickly identify the objectives to be pursued, the most important indications to observe and monitor, the possible developments in the situation and the plans of action to be followed. In other words, the assessment of the efficiency of the course of action which is selected (or better, automatically recalled in the memory) does not involve comparison with other actions but identifying directly a plausible, and hence satisfactory, solution. The decision-making models based on recognition [Klein, 1998] rely on the counter-intuitive observation that experts decide without analytically evaluating the pros and cons of each option (whereas non-experts decide on an analytical or comparative basis).

Using this model the decision-making process comprises three phases:

- evaluation of familiarity: the decision maker classes the problem as familiar or new, comparing it with other contexts encountered in the past;
- hypothesis building: if the context is classed as "new", additional information is sought or uncertainty is resolved by means of hypotheses (story-building) [Klein and Crandall, 1995] which can bring the problem within the framework of past experiences;
- assessment of alternatives: if the gap between the hypothesis (representation of the problem) and outcome is too great, the hypothesis is revised, together with the choices made to date.

In other words, when resources are extremely limited, the scenario is critical and the decision maker is an expert, he/she does not make any comparison between options, recognising a familiar context which is representative of a class of situations figuring in the long-term memory on the strength of very few indications or salient features.

When an expert takes a decision, he/she "photographs" the current situation and acts on the grounds of intuition deriving from past experience. The association between the observed indications and previous experience makes it possible to swiftly establish a possible course of action. Since in most cases the first option experts consider is reasonably acceptable, it is not necessary to generate [and subsequently compare] a large number of possible options, for the simple reason that cognitive processing would be entirely taken up with reckoning whether the chosen course of action can or cannot work with respect to the perceived scenario, without evaluating the pros and cons of two or more options. In this way, incidentally, greater control is maintained over the chosen course of action, for while a systematic comparison leads to an ideal solution and matches different solutions against one another, investing in a reasonable solution leaves the possibility open that this is not ideal and immutable but rather is imperfect, ensuring that the consequences are kept continually under close surveillance.

To sum up, the models based on recognition formalise the decision-making processes involved in expertise and intuitive decisions as follows [Klein, 1993 cf.]:

- identification of indications making it possible to recognise a pattern;
- the recognised pattern activates a scheme of action by association;
- the scheme of action is evaluated by means of mental simulation;
- the mental simulation is guided by a mental model [representation of a scenario's functioning].

A significant example is provided by the so-called circumstantial paradigm typical of medical semiotics. It is based not on analytical reasoning but on an intuitive activity enabling the medical expert to diagnose pathologies which are inaccessible to direct observation on the basis of superficial symptoms that are insignificant to the untrained eye. These are forms of knowledge which are prevalently mute, with rules that cannot readily be formulated and transmitted. No one will ever learn the art of diagnosis simply by referring to pre-existing rules. In this type of knowledge there are imponderable elements which come into play: flair, instinct, intuition. Some elements only reveal themselves to a scrupulous, practised observer, endowed with that "third eye" which is sometimes called a "clinical gaze" and which is developed in the course of time, through experience. It is one of the gifts of the expert: being able to make a correct diagnosis at a glance, in next to no time and with very few elements to go on.

In order to convert medical decisions into a rational process with the help of the theory of rational choice it would be necessary to go through the following stages:

- Each alternative X must be quantified according to the utility of each of its possible outcomes X1, X2, X3 etc. (for example, could be a delicate surgical operation which could result in a complete recovery, but could also leave the patient with permanent damage).

There are various methods for deriving these numeric values; some of them have the specific objective of obtaining values which reflect the personal preferences of the patient.

- The probability that each of the possible outcomes of the course of action   will come about must be determined. To this end the information available in the scientific literature – Evidence Based Medicine (EBM), which seeks to improve the quality of medical decisions by integrating the best scientific evidence with clinical experience and patients' values [Sackett *et al.*, 1997] – is clearly very important.

- The utility of each of the possible outcomes of has to be multiplied by the corresponding probability and the results totalled. This calculation gives the expected utility of X, and has to be made for each of the intervention alternatives considered. The alternative selected will be the one with the highest number, i.e. the one which maximizes the expected utility.

Nonetheless it is evident that the definition of formal criteria which in certain conditions make it possible to identify a choice as optimal does not throw any light on the real ability of the human mind to process the information and solve the problems. Numerous investigations and empirical researches – like the one published in 1992 in "Medical Decision Making" – clearly show that doctors and patients are not the rapid and efficient maximizers of utility contemplated by the theory of rational choice. As well as being often incompatible with the limits that cognitive structures and the complexity of the environment impose on human rationality, the formal methods do not take into consideration, on account of their difficulty of measurement, all the variables characterising clinical practice: suggestibility, beliefs, intuition, personal interest, emotions, memory and so forth. Moreover numerous experiments have shown that – even in the presence of high quality scientific information and data like those provided by the EBM – in many routine clinical decisions [for example the interpretation of a diagnostic test, the choice between different therapeutic options, the identification of a patient's preference, and so on] cognitive errors are commonly made.

Furthermore, even when both the exact percentage of error for a certain diagnostic test and the general frequency of an illness are known, doctors are often unable to infer the probability that a patient showing a positive outcome from a certain test actually has that illness. Gigerenzer [2003] has labelled "statistical illiteracy" the inability to interpret probabilistic problems and draw inferences based on Bayesian calculus. To give one example, Eddy [1982] asked a group of American doctors to assess the following problem:

One percent of 40 year old women taking part in a screening programme
have breast cancer. 80% of the women with breast cancer have a positive
mammogram. 9.69% of the women without breast cancer also have a
positive mammogram. A 40 year old women has just been screened and
has had a positive mammogram.
WHAT IS THE PROBABILITY THAT SHE HAS CANCER?

H and –H: represent the two hypotheses or possible results (presence of
breast cancer, absence of breast cancer).
D: data obtained (positive mammogram)
p (H/D): probability *a posteriori*. This probability can be calculated using
Bayes' theorem.

$$p(H/D) = \frac{p(H) \cdot p(D/H)}{p(H)\, p(D/H) + p(-H)\, p(D/-H)}$$

From the results it emerges that 95 interviewees out of 100 – including
medical experts, college students and personnel of the Harvard Medical
School [Casscells, Schoenberger and Grayboys, 1978] – believed that, in
view of the positive diagnostic test, the probability of the woman having
breast cancer was about 75%, ten times greater than the outcome when
Bayes' theorem is applied (7.8%). According to Gigerenzer and Hoffrage
[1995], these errors depend on the fact that a problem expressed in terms
of probability ignores the context in which people take decisions in
everyday life. In fact, information on general probability is rarely available in everyday life, and if it is made available it does not seem clear
because it is expressed in terms of abstract probabilities. If the probabilities are converted into natural frequency, the general information seems
more natural and would presumably be taken more into consideration.
To demonstrate their hypothesis, Hoffrage and Gigerenzer [1998] gave
two groups of participant the mammogram problem in terms of natural
frequency rather than probability.

> Eight out of every 1000 women have breast cancer. Of these 8
> women with breast cancer, 7 will have a positive mammogram. Of
> the remaining 992 women who don't have breast cancer, some 70
> will still have a positive mammogram. Imagine a sample of women
> who have positive mammograms in screening. How many of these
> women actually have breast cancer? [Gigerenzer, 2002, p. 42]

The results showed that even using the frequency format the task was
still hard to solve, but the manipulation of the format produced a substantial increase in the right answers, rising from 16% to 43%. Why should

this be so? The probability format got in the way of the "natural" rational approach to uncertainty. The representation in terms of natural frequency is a mental tool which makes it easier to come to a correct conclusion. One explanation is that for much of human history and evolution people have only dealt with natural frequency [Gigerenzer *et al.*, 1989]. Probabilities, percentages and other formal means of representing risk only began to emerge a few centuries ago as tools to measure degrees of uncertainty.

Fast and frugal heuristics

Gigerenzer [2001] has pointed out how, in terms of efficient behaviour, *homo heuristicus* loses out in comparison with *homo oeconomicus* only when the axioms and standards of normative rationality are involved. The capacity of individuals to make adaptive decisions – modifying their own cognitive strategies in relation to the context and to the structural mutations of the decision-making problem – provides the decision maker with a framework that is sufficiently optimistic in terms of the rationality of the behaviour [Payne, Bettman and Johnson 1993]. This inspired Gigerenzer to propose a revision of the classical concept of heuristics. If for Kahneman and Tversky heuristics are cognitive strategies (the cause of biases which compromise the making of correct decisions with regard to normative standards) for Gigerenzer heuristics are perfectly adaptive, "fast and frugal" rules which function within the constraints of the environment (limited time, insufficient information etc.) and the cognitive-computational limits of the decision maker [Tietz 1992]. The correspondence between the decision maker's mind and the environment is the turning point for an ecological redefinition of rationality [Todd and Gigerenzer 2000]. There are three fundamental rules for fast and frugal heuristics:

- The search rule: heuristics guide the search for information and alternatives within a limited timeframe (the search is not extensive as in the theory of rational choice) and without performing calculations;
- The stopping rule: this specifies how and when the search procedure must come to an end. In line with Simon's theory of bounded rationality, given the cognitive and environmental limits of real world problems, the search is ended on the basis of satisficing and not optimizing processes [Richardson 1998];
- The heuristic principle: fast and adaptive decision-making procedures which, despite their frugal nature, can be very accurate compared to classical algorithmic computation.

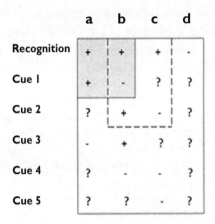

Figure 8 Take the Best Algorithm
[*Source*: Gigerenzer and Goldstein, 1996]

The so-called Take the Best heuristic, proposed by Gigerenzer [1997], outlines a satisficing choice criterion, although it is mostly used for choosing between two specific objects. This procedure is represented by a grid [Figure 8] in which the columns indicate the alternatives and the horizontal lines indicate the criteria or cues.

The alternatives (a, b, c, d) are examined two at a time through criteria or cues organized in a decreasing order on the basis of the validity that the agent assigns to them. The basic criterion is called recognition and is subjective. The following cues (in the example: cues 1-2-3-4-5) are of an ecological nature and are related to the specific context of the choice. In the example the values assigned to the cues are: positive (+), negative (–) or uncertain (?). The procedure works as follows. Let us suppose that we must choose which company, A or B, has the greater number of employees. On the basis of the first criterion (recognition) we must only "recognize (+) or not recognize (–) the object". We will suppose, as in the example, that we recognize both of the objects. In such a case, on the first line, recognition, we will have two + signs. At this point, because the criterion of identification does not allow us to distinguish between the two objects, we move on to consider the first "ecological" cue (cue 1): "the company has/does not have sub-units". We are aware of the fact that company A has sub-units and that company B does not (cue 1 line will have one + and one –). In such a case we do not need to proceed further: company A has more employees than company B. In other words, only four out of twelve values (the grey shaded area in Figure 8) were considered. Suppose at this point we have to repeat the whole procedure for objects B and C. As in the first case, both pass the recognition test (two

+ signs on the first line). The agent thus moves on to cue 1. In this case we know that company B does not have sub-units, but we do not know whether company C has any. In such a case we proceed to the second cue: for example "the company invests/does not invest in personnel retraining". We know that company B satisfies this cue (+) and that company C does not (–). At this point the criterion allows us to distinguish between the two objects and the process stops. Six out of twelve values [the area within the dotted line] have been considered. If, on the other hand, for the first criterion we had not recognized one of the two objects (C and D), the choice would have fallen to the recognized object and the process would have ended there. It is evident that if we do not recognize the object we cannot act on any cue (the column under the object C is in fact made up of only ?).

The decision-making process is therefore governed by an identification heuristic: the only condition necessary for making a choice is that one of the two available options has not been recognized. A criterion that allows for the differentiation between two objects is the best compared to other criteria.

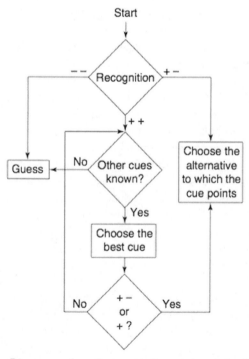

Figure 9 Flow Diagram of a Fast and Frugal heuristic: Take The Best [*Source:* Gigerenzer and Goldstein, 1996]

The distance between this approach and the inferential approach in which all of the available attributes are considered in a compensatory way is evident. Here there are no mathematical calculations to be performed or averages to be calculated, because the characteristics of each option are considered in a non-compensatory way. This type of "fast and frugal" heuristic search is based on a stopping rule called one reason, according to which the choice of an option is based on only one cue and on information that satisfies an optimal criterion for the decision maker. In such a case one can speak of ignorance-based decision making, which generally represents the first phase of all the one reason type decisions. The importance of this family of heuristics resides in the very type of ecological rationality implicit in their process. In line with Simon's structure, in particular with regards to the adaptive and procedural aspect with which agents choose their own courses of action, Gigerenzer proposes the metaphor of the Adaptive Toolbox [Gigerenzer 2001]. This is a sort of "toolbox" composed of a repertory of evolved heuristics which possess the following characteristics:

- they are specialized for certain tasks;
- from a computational point of view they are simple, frugal and fast;
- they do not have the problem of formal coherence, but rather that of adaptive efficiency;
- they solve on the spot problems related to the challenges presented by the environment (obtaining food, avoiding predators, finding a partner and a secure refuge, but also, at a higher level, exchanging goods, making a profit and so on).

Every individual chooses to use, as necessary, the heuristic best adapted to the task to be completed; during the completion of the task, the heuristic may also be substituted. In order to describe the nature of the "toolbox", Gigerenzer [2001] uses the image of a mechanic or sales person of used parts in a remote region who possesses neither the tools nor all the necessary spare parts, but who when faced with a problem tries to find a solution with the tools he has at his disposal. «These evolved capacities – explains Gigerenzer – are the metal from which the tools are made. A gut feeling is like a drill, a simple instrument whose force lies in the quality of its material» [2007, p. 63]. Such heuristics function well in natural situations, where the presence of limits in terms of time, knowledge and computational capacity make the adoption of fast and efficient strategies preferable. In reality, when liberated from their traditional negative connotations, heuristic strategies have become more than just deviations from a rational "norm". They respond to an ecological and adaptive rationality which allows individuals to efficiently face situations of uncertainty, risk and missing information typical of the reality in which we live.

Image theory

According to image theory, people's decisions are oriented by behavioural schemes or images made from the objectives and strategies used to achieve them [Beach and Mitchell, 1987]. To arrive at decisions people have recourse to both a set of self-images (values, ethic principles, beliefs, and so on) and images of trajectory, meaning the overall objectives, whether concrete or abstract, they wish to achieve in a certain context. The authors suggest that in order to achieve the established goals, people possess both images of the action, meaning mental schemes of the actions to be performed, and projected images, meaning anticipations and forecasts of future events and states. Within this theory it is possible to identify two major categories of decision:

1. Adoption decisions, involving the acquisition of new objectives which must be compatible with those already existing in the mind of the decision maker;
2. Progress decisions, determining whether the decision-making process is progressing towards the established goals.

One of the fundamental mechanisms of the decision-making process is the analysis of the compatibility which determines the threshold beyond which an alternative is defined compatible or incompatible with the image classes. Suppose that a couple decide to buy a new house costing more than they can afford. Their objective will be to obtain the necessary sum of money, and they decide to do odd jobs to earn the money. At a certain point they realise that this is not enough and they modify the plan, having recourse for example to a loan. The decision is compatible with their values and enables them to reach the established goal [Beach and Mitchell, 1987].

There are two mechanisms in play:

- Control of compatibility, evaluating the compatibility between the decision-making options and the criteria laid down by the various images (schemes). For example, if the image of the current trajectory is not very compatible with the image of the original project, the decision makers will have to change their plan (negative outcome of the progress decision). If the recourse to a loan (from a bank or friends) contradicts the principle (self-image) "do not have debts", the couple will not choose the loan as a project but will go on working until they have enough money available;

- Control of the options advantage: the options which have passed the control of compatibility have to be subjected to competitive analysis. In fact several decision-making options may have been adjudged to be compatible. The control of advantage makes it possible to choose the best of the remaining options and focus on the value of the outcomes. At this point the image theory incorporates the previous theories. The control of advantage uses such strategies as calculation of expected value, decision-making heuristics, calculation of probabilities, and so on.

The image theory highlights the dynamic and adaptive aspects of behaviour: decision making consists in a continuous reconsideration of the state of progress towards a specific goal. On the basis of the results obtained in the field of Naturalistic Decision Making, Lipshitz and Strauss [1997] carried out numerous studies of the way in which individuals cope with uncertainty in "natural" contexts, meaning situations characterised by inadequate understanding, incomplete information and undifferentiated alternatives. They formulated the RAWFS heuristic (Reduction, Assumption-based reasoning, Weighing, Forestalling and Suppressing uncertainty) which sums up the way decision makers tackle uncertainty without having recourse to calculations or the RQP heuristic. In other words, to cope with uncertainties decision makers use the following five principal strategies:

- Reduction: they try to reduce the uncertainty by trying to obtain information;
- Assumption-based reasoning: they try to make good the information shortfalls by drawing on previous knowledge or imagination;
- Weighing: they assess the pros and cons of the various options (an approximate version of the model of expected utility);
- Forestalling: they devise a course of action to contrast any negative contingencies, for example by preparing alternative plans of action for the worst-case scenarios;
- Suppressing uncertainty: for example, by ignoring it or taking risky decisions.

HUMAN INFERENCES

Intuition as a Strategy of Natural Logic

The Anti-Psychologism of Formal Logic

The science of the lògos (from the Greek λόγος in its dual meaning of "word" and "reason"), providing a rational justification for discourse and valid inferences, first received a systematic formulation in Aristotle's *Organon*. The Greek philosopher used the term 'analytic' for the science that analyses and breaks down thought into its constituent elements in order to appraise its validity. Down the centuries the syllogism (from συν together", and λογος "reasoning") – a sequence comprising two premisses and a conclusion designed to establish the necessary relationship between the propositions – has stood as the canonical form of deductive reasoning.

In its reflexive sense the Aristotelian lògos refers not to the mental processes – which he defines as "affects of the soul" – but to their objective contents, the judgements which have their linguistic equivalent in utterances. It is the inference itself, not the process of drawing inferences, that constitutes the object of study of logic. Logic is not to concern itself with the psychological processes at work while we are reasoning: these are the subject of psychology. Instead it must study the structure of reasoning, the truth of the propositions, and the consequential link between premisses and conclusions. Many centuries later Aristotle's attempt to probe the utterances of natural language inspired some enquiring minds in the 19th and 20th centuries to try to penetrate the dynamics of the reasoning employed in mathematical demonstrations. This paved the way for a grand revival in logic's fortunes, with the help of the more powerful and rigorous conceptual tool of mathematics.

One of the fundamental pioneers of modern logic was Leibniz. Writing in the middle of the 17th century, he pursued the dream of constructing a *calculus ratiocinator* devoid of any psychological or subjective conditioning, able to reduce human reasoning to the mere manipulation of symbols in the *characteristica universalis*, a sort of "alphabet of human thoughts" which would make it possible to arrive at rational conclusions, just as for problems of arithmetic and geometry.

> [...] quando orientur controversiae, non magis disputatione opus erit inter duos philosophos, quam inter duos Computistas. Sufficiet enim calamos in manus sumere sedereque ad abacos, et sibi mutuo [accito si placet amico] dicere: calculemus! [Leibniz, 1890, vol. 7, p. 200]

Although Leibniz's project had great potential, some two centuries went by before the emergence of mathematical logic. The first attempt to express the laws of thought by means of rules and symbolic operations was made by Boole. Reacting against the traditional view that the syllogism was the only valid process for logical reasoning, Boole demonstrated that the laws of thought could constitute a coherent system even without using that standard sequence, and bear more of a resemblance to algebra. The hypothesis of a concordance between the laws of thought and those of algebra led him to claim that the salient laws pertained to the major mental faculties, and that mathematics spoke directly about human intelligence. To put it another way, Boole provided the logical tool for representing the laws of thought by means of mathematical calculus and its symbolisation, which would make it possible to formulate logical deduction as if it were "calculation".

The progressive development of mathematical logic, mirroring the structure of the laws governing mental activity, received a fundamental impulse from Frege, the founder of modern logic. To avoid confusion, Frege distinguished between thought (*Gedanke*), in the sense of logical content, and thinking (*Denken*). By placing the emphasis on thinking rather than its representations, Frege widened the distance from psychology. In *Ideography* [1879] and subsequently in *The Foundation of Arithmetic* [1884], he drew on Leibniz in propounding the idea of a "writing of concepts", a language of pure thought expressed in formulae which, unlike natural language, can provide a rigorous and definitive solution to the problem of what lies at the heart of arithmetic. Thus the theory of thought (or "logic" as he preferred to call it) had to institute a logical language (or "ideography") able to free mental structures – seen as objective thought rather than subjective mental activity – from their grammatical garb and the inadequacy of traditional logic. This objective was the first step towards a profound reassessment of the nature of mathematics in purely logical terms. Only in this way would it be possible to grasp those 'objects' of arithmetic which are not perceived through the senses but belong from the outset in the domain of reason.

> No, arithmetic has nothing at all to do with sensations. Just as little has it to do with mental images, compounded from the traces of earlier sense impressions. The fluctuating and indeterminate nature of these forms stands in stark contrast to the determinate and fixed nature of mathematical concepts and objects. [*The Frege Reader*, Frege and Beaney, p. 87]

In his anti-psychological stand, Frege contrasts subjective representations with what is purely objective, thought and shared by everybody. He speaks of numbers as objects which are independent of thought, just as the laws of nature were not invented but simply discovered.

If the task of logic is to work on pure thought, there is no need to enquire into its psychic process. Logic has to distinguish what is logical from what lies outside this sphere. Thoughts, according to Frege, not only have no need to be recognised as such to be true, but their truth is independent of the fact that we think them. Thought is not the object of psychology; it does not consist in representations in the psychological sense. The thought expressed by the theorem of Pythagoras is the same for everybody, standing out immutable in all its objectivity. On the contrary, each individual has their own representations, sensations, sentiments, which belong to them and them alone. We grasp thoughts, we do not create them. In fables and in poetry there are thoughts which are neither true nor false, whereas in logic a thought has to be either true or false: *tertium non datur* [Frege, 1906].

In contrasting the act of thinking and the object of thought, Frege alludes to Plato's ontology: thoughts are no longer merely objective elements, but entities belonging to a third realm. They are distinct from subjective representations which, in order to exist, require the presence of someone with changing, incommunicable moods that affect their thoughts.

The Fallacy of Universal Logic

Since Frege, the idea that it is the task of logic to establish the laws for drawing correct inferences has placed the emphasis squarely on deductive inference. In reality, in our day to day reasoning and adaptations inference plays only a marginal role. On account of the limits of their cognitive processes and the problems posed by the environment, human beings cannot elaborate long sequences of deductive inferences, which in any case do not produce new knowledge. However, in the interests of adaptation and survival, a logic of justification is not enough: a logic of discovery is required. More often than not our reasoning is based on inferences which are not necessarily deductive, propositional or conscious. This means that the concept of natural logic goes beyond what is implicit in traditional formal logic [Cellucci, 2008]. Formal, classic logic has to be set in a more wide-ranging conceptual framework which, far from weakening it, will actually make it more powerful.

An initial distinction between natural and formal logic was formulated by philosophers during the Renaissance. The principle of inferential deduction was believed to have been laid down by nature, and that accordingly formal logic was modelled on natural logic. In fact, if the latter came into being at the same time as human beings and is rooted in their minds [Ramo, 1964b], formal logic, introduced by humans, should merely observe and imitate as closely as possible the innate rules existing in human minds [Ramo, 1964a]. This relationship between natural logic (the fruit of biological evolution) and formal logic (the fruit of cultural evolution) persisted into the first half of the 18th century. Then the relationship became oppositive, as the idea that formal logic was the only possible type of logic came to predominate. Kant affirmed that logic is the science of the necessary, universal rules of thought, and that these rules can be known *a priori*, independently of the natural use of the intellect [Kant, 1919]. Besides, if logic were not innate, Locke argued, no one before Aristotle would have discovered anything by means of reason, and only those expert in logic would be able to reason correctly. In fact the intellect has an innate ability to recognise the coherence and incoherence of its ideas, even though it knows nothing of syllogisms [Locke, 1690].

According to Frege, only formal logic – the science of the general laws of truth – can indicate the correct procedures the intellect has to adopt in order to think and thus be prescriptive. Natural logic, on the contrary, is descriptive because it explains the processes of thought and judgement by referring to subjective truths. Our judgements, in fact, act on the basis of psychological laws, meaning that they can lead to truth but also to error [Frege, 1969]: thus logic must necessarily exclude these considerations from its field of enquiry. The task of logic is to give us norms that will lead us to the truth.

In reality, the rules of natural logic are at one and the same time descriptive and prescriptive. Just as medicine prescribes appropriate therapies to enable the patient to regain health – therapies that are in any case based on a description of the functioning of certain bodily processes – so natural logic prescribes rules for solving problems, rules which are also based on a description of the functioning of certain "bodily processes", but in this case processes of reasoning [Cellucci, 2008].

It is surely more plausible to imagine the existence of a multiplicity of logics rather than a formal universal logic. Gödel's *theorem of incompleteness* demonstrates that no logical system can cover all logical truths. Besides, if it is true that the laws of natural logic are not always true because they have been generated during the tortuous evolutionary process of the human species, then the same goes for formal logic, on account of its link with the cognitive architectures of the human mind, framed during the same evolutionary process [Maldonato and Dell'Orco, 2010].

This shows just how close a link exists between logic and the pursuit of means for survival. Traditionally, on the contrary, logic was considered a superior faculty, exclusive to human beings and enabling them to overcome those limits of their biological make-up which constitute inescapable restrictions for non humans and plants. In particular, such a faculty would have a direct counterpart in certain original truths and certain fundamental principles required for any instance of demonstrative reasoning. But reason is not a superior faculty. True to the original meaning of *ratio*, it is the ability to choose the most appropriate means for the goals being pursued. In this sense nothing is rational in itself but only in relation to a goal.

The Asymmetries of Rationality and the Crisis of the Logico-Formal System

It was during the Enlightenment that the controversy over the nature of human rationality came to a head. Over the centuries the term "rational" has had different meanings, indicating reason itself, reasonableness, a domain covering the form and procedures of reason, and a principle of coherence between a system of values and the objectives adopted [Braine, 1978]. For those studying the theory of decision making, rationality concerns the choice of the most appropriate means and behaviour for achieving predetermined aims. Rationality is based on the criteria of coherence between thought and action and between means and end; the transitivity that makes it possible to move from the project to its accomplishment by evaluating preferences according to their functionality and optimization so as to achieve the goal through the least possible use of means. This, of course, requires both as much information as possible on the viable alternatives and a certain degree of creativity, above all when there is a significant disparity between the possibilities of information, and its processing, and the complexity of the current situation [Bencivenga, 1985]. Reasoning, on the other hand, can be defined as a system of procedures: of inference, argumentation, conclusion, induction, deduction, analogy and more besides. In other words, it is the set of mental processes by means of which we draw inferences and elaborate new knowledge on the basis of given knowledge.

Traditionally reasoning has been divided up into two categories: deductive, when one passes from the general to the particular, and inductive, when one passes from the particular to the general. If one considers the nature of the information featuring in the knowledge possessed *a priori*, one can say that in deductive inferences the conclusions are already implicitly present in the specific premises. This means that no new knowledge is generated; rather, something implicitly known is expressed in a different manner. On the contrary, in inductive inferences the conclusion does not feature in the specific premises, and it reveals something about the reality that was not previously known. It is clear that here, unlike with the deductive inferences, one cannot draw valid conclusions from a logical standpoint [Lemmon, 2008]. A further element of classification concerns the nature of the premises. Before drawing an inference the premises may be affirmations which are absolutely certain or with a certain margin of certainty. In the latter case we are dealing with probabilistic reasoning. A probabilistic inference may be either deductive or inductive. In fact there are four categories of non-probabilistic deductive reasoning. In terms of our enquiry the mechanisms of reasoning which underlie decision making are of importance, for this is an activity involving both probabilistic and deductive inferences [Girotto, 1994]. The process of logic's "de-psychologization", designed to banish ambiguities, imprecisions and individual subjectivity, made a big impact on the first generation of cognitive scientists, convinced that the study of the properties of formal systems could constitute a valid criterion also for investigating the correct functioning of mental mechanisms. Among the various theories of reasoning we shall consider here those of mental logic and mental models, and the heuristics and biases programme.

Theory of mental logic

The mind comprises formal schemes of inference which, independently of the content of the premises, lead to valid conclusions. In reality this theory returns to Aristotle's identification of logic and thought, which remained a cardinal idea up until the mid-19th century, when the rules of formal logic still constituted the normative parameter for analysing the human mind. For centuries the most reliable approach was seen as referring to the laws of logic as the basis for psychological analysis of thought, in line with the science of logic inaugurated by Aristotle.

However, these norms only represent a small part of thought in its entirety. Wundt [1912] argued that any attempt to explain thought starting from the laws of logic can only lead to a distortion of the real facts, confining them to an inextricable and fruitless tangle which is extraneous to the real psychological processes. Yet in its infancy, the psychology of reasoning identified human thought with formal logic, postulating that people's minds, whether or not they are expert in logic, are endowed with a sort of mental logic able to make valid inferences. For example, people are capable of drawing the valid inference of the *modus ponens* (e.g. «All men are mortal», «Socrates is a man», therefore «Socrates is mortal») because they apply the corresponding scheme, which they unconsciously possess, to the premisses. This explanation is undoubtedly easy to accept, given its intuitive nature and formal elegance. Nonetheless there are at least two classes of phenomenon which it is unable to account for: 1) false inferences from premisses that would consent the application of schemes of valid inferences; 2) the influence of the content of the premisses on the inferences. To overcome these difficulties, some alternative theories to mental logic have been developed over the last two decades. The discovery of errors of reasoning, above all from the 1970s onwards, dealt a severe blow to the most radical versions of the theory of mental logic, such as Piaget's theory, whereby cognitive development culminates with the acquisition of all the rules of propositional logic [Inhelder and Piaget, 1955]. This setback favoured the elaboration of alternative versions of the theory in which the rules of inference are applied to the premisses according to the way in which they are interpreted by the agents on the basis of semantic and pragmatic processes. In fact, although by definition a scheme of formal logic tends to lead to the same inferences irrespective of the content of the premisses to which it is applied, in reality people's inferences vary widely according to the content of the premisses and the context in which they are presented, even if the logical form of the premisses remains unchanged.

Theory of mental models

This theory was formulated as a result of the pioneering work of Johnson-Laird [1983]. It involves a notion of mental representation based on the assumption that people do not possess a mind which comes ready equipped with formal rules of inference. They are able to understand the premisses of a reasoning not on the basis of the application of an inferential method but starting from the construction and manipulation of mental representations (models). In other words, our thought processes are not based on events in the external world or in our mind but on descriptions of events in the form of mental representations influenced both by the description of the events and by the functional limits of the human mind. This would account for many "mental blanks", those oversights and distractions which contribute to causing major and minor accidents. According to Johnson-Laird the errors can be explained by the restrictions imposed by the limits of our working memory. This theory, which was initially elaborated for deductive reasoning, has subsequently been applied also to inductive and decisional reasoning. The theory of mental models has thrown light on the illusions of reasoning and on those illusory inferences which the theory of mental logic does not account for. In fact only valid inferences can be drawn from logical rules, meaning inferences which always lead to true conclusions if the premises are true, and false conclusions if the premises are false (irrespective of the content of the premises). The fact that people who are not expert draw valid or false inferences does not depend on the presence or absence of a given inferential scheme in their mind but on the greater or lesser degree of complexity of the representation required to be able to retrieve it. According to such a theory, the more models have to be elaborated to arrive at a valid conclusion, the more difficult the inferential process.

At this point we must ask: can the principles of scientific rationality be considered useful approximations of human reasoning? Furthermore, if the theory of rational choice is plausible, why do people fail to abide by it, sometimes systematically? Since the middle of the 20th century it has become steadily clearer that rationality is not governed by cognitive structures of unlimited computational power. Researchers have tried to develop a more realistic theory of rational behaviour, toning down the classical criteria of optimization. Further restrictions on the application of the principles of rationality are also due to the imperfection of the contexts in which choices and reasoning take place. In fact, it is hardly ever the case that all the information required for optimal knowledge is available: on the contrary, we are often up against situations of uncertainty and/or lack of information. Let us suppose, for example, we have to buy a bottle of wine. If our objective were to choose the best possible bottle, we would have to taste the wine from each bottle and opt for the best. Evidently few people are willing to follow such a procedure. In most cases, when confronted by uncertainty we rely on the rules we have acquired through experience or common sense: colour, year, label and so forth. It is not certain that such rules will ensure good choices, but they are convenient and not infrequently they prove to be perfectly satisfactory.

Heuristics and biases programme

While the two theories outlined above are traditionally applied to deductive reasoning, this programme, formulated in 1982 by Kahneman, Slovic and Tversky, is used for the analysis of probabilistic reasoning. As we have already seen, in such an approach the inferences of non experts depend on the activation of non systematic problem solving procedures – heuristics – which do not necessarily guarantee a normatively correct solution. Indeed, in many cases they lead to systematic errors (biases). Clearly any general theory dealing with reasoning is not immune to theoretical problems. In this specific case, there are basically three such errors. In the first place, the problem of competence. It used to be thought that, even if people lacked specific knowledge in the field of formal logic, they were nonetheless able to apply it when engaged in reasoning. However, it now appears that, contrary to the normative principles of logic and statistics [Johnson-Laird, 1983], the inferences we make, whether in day to day situations or in experimental conditions, are subject to numerous systematic errors. The second problem concerns how these errors can be accounted for. And thirdly, the effect on reasoning of the content of the premisses and the context in which they are presented: agents behave differently when confronted with problems which, while having the same formal structure, are presented in different forms. Strategies and hypotheses are also affected by expectations and the way in which the task is presented.

These affirmations are borne out by the well-known experiment devised by Wason [1960] known as the *four-card selection task*. Participants were shown the following four cards:

Each card has a letter on one side and a number on the other. Participants were informed of the rule that if a card has a vowel on one side, it must have an even number on the other. The task is to say how many cards need to be turned over in order to verify whether this rule holds good or not. The correct answer, rarely given, is to turn over only two cards: card E and card 7. In fact, if on the back of E there is an odd number, the rule is false; if on the back of 7 there is a vowel, again the

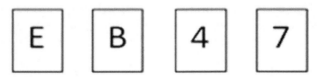

Figure 10 Four-Card Selection Test

rule is false. In other words, any card with a vowel on one side and an odd number on the other breaks the rule. On the contrary, opting for card 4 and card B, the ones most often chosen by participants, is pointless because the rule states "if there is a vowel then there is an even number" and not "only if" there is a vowel, so that on the other side of 4 there could be either a vowel or a consonant, just as on the other side of B there could be either an odd or an even number. This experiment demonstrates the tendency, very common in inferential tasks, to acquire information which only goes to confirm a hypothesis, without checking the falsifying cases. In other words, it is not sufficient to know the hypotheses: one must also taken into account the expectations.

Formal logic has been considered as underpinning not only the sciences and mathematics – where correct reasoning inevitably follows logical procedures and canons – but also day to day reasoning. The divergence between natural logic and formal logic – meaning the mind's ability to solve problems and acquire new knowledge and the formal theory of deductive inference – has been the subject of extensive experimental investigation by cognitive scientists, who have demonstrated the limits of human inferential capacity. In fact, if at first it was believed that humans possess an innate logical competence, and that our inferential errors derive only from a defective application of the rules of inference on account of our biological, cognitive and possibly also social limits [Manktelow and Over, 1990], nowadays researchers recognise an intrinsic difference between our natural logic and formal logic. The latter, investing only a part of our thought – i.e. the production of rational arguments in support of a thesis – does not succeed in explaining all the innumerable nuances of this thought. In fact thinking also means sensing, imagining and elaborating hypotheses, and many more things besides.

Today we still do not possess an algorithm able to translate a "real" line of argument into natural language. In everyday life the validity of an argument is important, but we usually evaluate it without having recourse to logic. Not being able to predict the actual behaviour of human beings, the rules of logic cannot accurately describe the mechanisms underlying reasoning. In meeting the challenges which continually confront us in life, there is very little in common between *action readiness* [Frijda, Manstead and Bem, 2000] and the algorithms of classical logic. The logico-formal model is beset by the uncertainty, emotions, gut sensations and impulses to act with which evolution has endowed us to cope with life's emergencies. Certainly one can take a decision by using the strategies of formal reasoning. In the great majority of choices, however, above all in situations of uncertainty and risk, the brain does not adopt Bayes's models of inference – highly laborious and not always adaptable to the specific decision-making problems – but a sort of natural logic whose rules, while being undoubtedly less rigorous and fallible, have proved to be more adaptable and effective throughout the course of human development. The great adaptive value of our emotional repertoire, linked above all to speed of action, shows itself to be fundamental in situations of danger or circumstances in which hesitating or reflecting on what to do could be fatal. Undoubtedly if our emotions kept a hold over our brain and body for any length of time – irrespective of how circumstances evolved – they would be poor guides to action. It is in fact much more "economic" to rely on certain physical signals which can alert us in an instant to cope with an emergency rather than analysing complex situations in every detail. If our ancestors – in order to meet the challenges of a hostile, unknown and in many respects unpredictable environment – had had recourse to the subtle and sophisticated geometries of reason, we would surely not be here today to chart the distance we have come. Nowadays the pressures faced by human populations at the dawn of civilization have eased off, but the "emotional mind" continues to be our radar in identifying danger [Goleman, 1996]. As for heuristics, the emotions elude the typical analytic reflection of the "rational" mind, manifesting themselves much more rapidly, to the point that they do not even cross the threshold of consciousness [Ekman, 1992].

Rational Gut Feeling

Rational thought was long considered to be an activity governed by formal laws designed to maximize expected utility. Yet most of our day to day decisions are based on mental processes which have nothing to do with logic. Everybody will have expressed a judgement or taken a decision trusting in their own gut feelings: «I don't trust that person», «my sixth sense tells me not to take the risk», «I sensed a bargain» and so on. Gigerenzer relates the amusing anecdote of a philosophy professor at Columbia University found racking his brains trying to decide whether to accept an offer from a rival university or stay where he was. A colleague simply said: «Just maximize your expected utility—you always write about doing this." Exasperated, the first philosopher responded: "Come on, this is serious"» [Gigerenzer and Todd, 1999, p. 9].

Contrary to the received wisdom of economics manuals, it is often gut feelings, emotions or intuition which induce people to make those sudden, spontaneous outbursts – «I know what I'll do!» or «That's my best choice!» – which actually manifest judicious rationality. By itself formal logic will never be able to tell us who to marry, who to trust, or even which job to choose; in such cases Plato's charioteer is invariably governed by his emotional horses [Lehrer, 2009].

While the analysis of decision-making received little attention for a very long time, the same cannot be said for the study of human intuition. Already in the first half of the 20th century Gestalt psychologists were focusing on the phenomenon of rapid problem solving and intuition in particular [Bastick, 1982; Bowers *et al.*, 1990]. Recent studies have shown how, above all in conditions of discriminative uncertainty, perception has recourse to stratagems which resemble heuristic judgements. In fact perception means eliminating the ambiguities, choosing one interpretation rather than another: in short, deciding [Berthoz, 2006]. Take, for example, visual perception: this is not a mechanical faculty but a probabilistic function that enables us to obtain a unitary representation (*unitas multiplex*) of the retinal images which are for ever changing their form, size, luminosity and so on as a result of both environmental variations and internal neuro-physiological dynamics. In conditions of uncertainty, our perceptive system, just like our intuitive judgement, goes beyond the information received and "gambles" that matters stand in a certain fashion [Gigerenzer, 2005]. Thanks to perceptive constancy, for example, we are able to perceive an object more or less as it really is, even in conditions which deform it. This is a highly adaptive process: it would be a great waste of psychic energy to be constantly regulating our perceptive abilities; indeed we would probably lapse into a state of inertia.

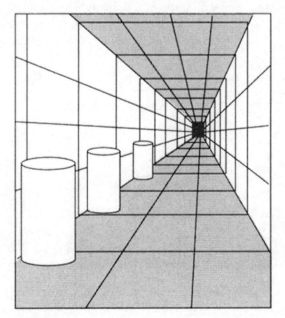

Figure 11 Retinal Image and Distance
[*Source*: Kanizsa, 1979]

Moreover the constancy of size enables us to perceive objects as always being the same size: when we see a person or an object in the distance, however small the retinal image we do not think that they are small but rather that they are a long way away [Figure 11]. This means that, in a wholly automatic fashion, our brain has compensated for the variations in size of the retinal image resulting from variations in distance.

Another constancy, that of form, enables us to perceive objects as always having the same shape, even though the retinal image changes according to the angle of observation. If, for example, we observe a door which is closed, open or ajar, even though its rectangular form goes through a series of trapezoidal distortions our visual system takes into account the depth and distance, inferring entirely automatically that what we are perceiving is always a rectangular door moving on its hinges. Perception operates a constant series of unconscious inferences [von Helmholtz, 1967] vis-à-vis nature and the environment in which our brain has evolved. For example, given that the main light sources in our environment, the sun and moon, are positioned above the objects being lit up, the unconscious inference when confronted with figures A and B [Figure 12] is that, if the shadow is in the upper part, the dots are set into the surface and are convex. Vice versa, if the shadow is in the lower part, the dots protrude from the surface and are thus concave.

In other words, although the retinal image is bi-dimensional, the brain takes into account the information on light and shade to deduce in which direction the dots are protruding and in practice invents a third

A   **B**

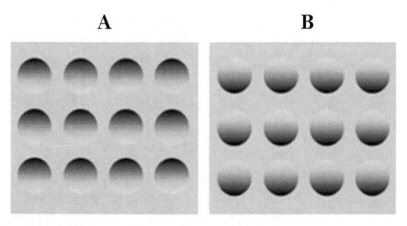

Figure 12 Perceptual illusion of "pop-out" dots. If you turn the page around, the concave dots will pop out and vice versa. The right picture is identical to the left, rotated by 180 degrees.
[*Source*: Gigerenzer, 2008, p. 67]

dimension, framing the scenario that is most likely in the external world [Montague, 2006]. The demonstration that such an inference is not unequivocal lies in the fact that, turning the book upside down, the dots in A appear concave and those in B convex. Our brain completes the physical world and goes beyond the information received, enabling us to adapt to the environment around us.

To give another example, in everyday life we see objects which are partly hidden (a person sitting at a desk, a dog behind a tree with only the head and tail visible, and so on) and yet we perceive them as wholes. We need to give sense to the environment around us. Thus when the sensorial stimuli are incomplete or devoid of sense, we slightly alter them, drawing on mnemonic or fantastic material so that the whole perceptive experience becomes significant. This perception, which goes beyond sensorial information, represents a decision taken by the brain, a way of "filling in the gaps" which ensures the coherence of our perception of the world. For example, in one of the best known illusions in Gestalt psychology, Kanizsa's triangle [Figure 13], the brain completes the outlines of the triangles with outlines that, despite being perceived, do not exist in the physical world.

These illusions, together with others in different spheres of visual perception, give an effective demonstration of how our brain tends to complete the physical world. As a matter of fact we can also find ourselves victims of illusions which do not concern the traditional five senses. These may be to do with time, as when we perceive an effect before its cause, indicating considerable flexibility in our mental software which has only recently been identified. Again, we can perceive someone as being more trustworthy than his actual behaviour suggests. And when it comes to falling in love, the mind can construct a person who practically does

Figure 13 Kanizsa Triangle. The illusory triangle appears brighter than its surround and is delineated by an illusory edge.
[*Source*: Kanizsa, 1979].

not exist – friends on the sidelines commonly remain stunned that we cannot "see" the bad character that lurks behind the romantic image [Montague, 2006].

Psychologists have related a whole series of phenomena to the concept of intuition as an instinctive mental faculty: spontaneous inferences, unconscious perceptions, tacit knowledge, experiential knowledge, emotional intelligence, heuristics and even creativity and the "sixth sense". Such a vast range of phenomena has actually made the definition of "intuition" all too vague. Epstein [1991], for example, defines this automatic, associative, holistic, non verbal process as experiential, acting on the basis of rapid associations with past experiences deposited in our long-term memory. On the contrary, rational thought is a process of conscious, deliberative, analytic and verbal reasoning. This table [Figure 14] sums up the fundamental features of Epstein's Cognitive Experiential Self-Theory (CEST).

Simon [1955] was one of the first to argue that the deliberations of the

EXPERIENTIAL SYSTEM (An automatic learning system)	RATIONAL SYSTEM (A conscious reasoning system)
1. Preconscious	1. Conscious
2. Automatic	2. Deliberative
3. Concrete: Encodes reality in images, metaphors, and narratives	3. Abstract: Encodes reality in symbols, words, and numbers
4. Holistic	4. Analytic
5. Associative: Connections by similarity and contiguity	5. Cause-and-effect relations
6. Intimately associated with affect	6. Affect-free
7. Operates by hedonic principle (what feels good)	7. Operates by reality principle (what is logical and supported by evidence)
8. Acquires its schemas by learning from experience	8. Acquires its beliefs by conscious learning and logical inference
9. Outcome oriented	9. More process oriented
10. Behaviour mediated by "vibes" from past experience	10. Behaviour mediated by conscious appraisal of events
11. Rapid processing: Oriented toward immediate action	11. Slower processing: Capable of long delayed action
12. Resistant to change: Changes with repetitive or intense experience	12. Less resistant to change: Can change with speed of thought
13. Crudely differentiated: Broad generalization gradient; categorical thinking	13. More highly differentiated nuanced thinking
14. Crudely integrated: situationally specific; organized in part by cognitive-affective modules	14. More highly integrated: Organized in part by cross-situational principles
15. Experienced passively and preconsciously: We are seized by our emotions	15. Experienced actively and consciously: We believe we are in control of our thoughts
16. Self-evidently valid: "Experiencing is believing"	16. Requires justification via logic and evidence

Figure 14 Epstein's Cognitive Experiential Self-Theory (CEST). [*Source:* Epstein, 1991]

human mind are guided by rapid and adaptive intuitive processes, performed with little apparent effort and without (or almost without) conscious deliberation. He had this to say about intuition: It is an observable fact that people sometimes reach solutions to problems suddenly. They then have an "aha!" experience of varying degrees of intensity. There is no doubt of the genuineness of the phenomenon. Moreover, the problem solutions people reach when they have these experiences, when they make intuitive judgments, frequently are correct [Simon, 1983, p. 201]. Intuitive thought processes, in a few seconds and without any conscious effort, a large amount of information deposited in our long-term memory, in practice carrying out an immediate recognition of the current situation which is satisficing [Simon, 1955] and often reliable on the grounds of analogies. In whatever field people have achieved note-worthy levels of experience, a large number of stimuli will have been accumulated that can be recognised by simple "gut feelings". One can think, for example, of a chess grandmaster who only needs to observe a situation for a few seconds to be able to come up with a decisive move that is often the best possible one in that situation [Simon, 1979].

Every professional entomologist has a comparable ability to discriminate among the insects he sees, and every botanist among the plants. In any field of expertise, possession of an elaborate

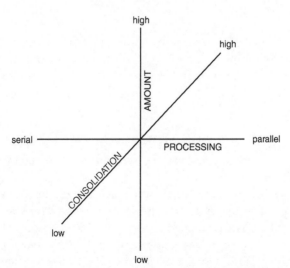

Figure 15 Characteristics of processing strategies in judgment and decision making. Intuitive strategies fall into the upper right quadrant.
[*Source*: Betsch, 2008]

discrimination net that permits recognition of any one of tens of thousands of different objects or situations is one of the basic tools of the expert and the principal source of his intuitions. [Simon, 1983, p. 26]

The psychology of decision making commonly identifies intuition with heuristics [Gilovich, Griffin and Kahneman, 2002], meaning unmediated mental strategies which, by means of parallel processing, simplify and speed up judgements and decisions. However, although they are rapid and able to retrieve large quantities of information deposited in the memory, the parallel processes ignore the weight of new data because they are strongly influenced by knowledge that has already been consolidated. The axes of the table in Figure 15 show the quantity of information, style of processing and degree of consolidation.

A well-trained brain knows which details to look for [Lehrer, 2009]. Take a professional baseball player. What enables him to catch or strike a ball? In both cases the player uses a set of automatic rules of thumb.

When a man throws a ball high in the air and catches it again, he behaves as if he had solved a set of differential equations in predicting the trajectory of the ball. He may neither know nor care what a differential equation is, but this does not affect his skill with the ball. At some subconscious level, something functionally equivalent to the mathematical calculation is going on. [Dawkins, 1989, p. 96]

Before the ball has been thrown the brain has already assimilated information needed to foresee how it will fly through the air. A torqued wrist suggests a curveball, while an elbow fixed at a right angle means that a fastball is coming, straight over the plate. Two fingers on the seam might indicate a slider, and a ball gripped with the knuckles is a sure sign that a wavering knuckleball is on its way. The batters, of course, aren't consciously studying these signs; they can't tell you why they decided to swing at certain pitches. And yet, they are able to act based on this information [Lehrer, 2009].

When the ball is in the air, expert players, without generally being aware of it [McBeath et al., 2002], use a sort of visual heuristic: keep your eye on the ball, start to run and regulate your speed keeping the angle of vision constant, meaning the angle between the eye and the ball with respect to the ground. Using this rule the player does not need to assess the wind, air resistance, the rotation effect or other variables because all the relevant facts are already included in a single variable: the angle of vision [Gigerenzer, 2008]. If the ball is not yet stationary, the player will keep his eye on it, start to run and this time regulate his speed so that the image of the ball rises at a constant speed.

> One can intuitively see its logic. If the player sees the ball rising from the point it was hit with accelerating speed, he had better run backward because the ball will meet the ground behind his present position. If, however, the ball rises with decreasing speed, he needs to run toward the ball instead. If the ball rises at a constant speed, the player is in the right position. [Gigerenzer, 2008, p. 88]

From an evolutionary standpoint, the techniques of interception of objects have had a highly adaptive value. Take hunting: in order to kill prey with a spear, stone or bow, it was fundamental to be able to foresee the animal's trajectory. Similarly, to survive in case of attacks by animals (such as a bird of prey swooping down from above) or other humans (perhaps throwing stones or sticks)it was a matter of life or death to be able to carry out an effective telemetric examination so as to dodge the object. In this sense intuition is a highly ecological tool: it provides immediate, efficacious responses at low levels of cognitive expenditure.

There is no doubt that if reason is not used, intuitive thought can be misleading and imprecise. Yet we do not err only by trusting to instinct: we also make mistakes when we think too rationally and take a long time reflecting on what actions to take, because we "choke" our gut feelings and emotions, depriving ourselves of their innate wisdom.

This choking effect can be harmful, for example, for an artist or a professional athlete [Baumeister, 1984]. Beginners have to focus on their performance in order to execute a technical gesture correctly, but for professionals, increasing the level of attention in a process which has already become automatic may be counterproductive [Beilock et al., 2004]. When they perform in conditions of psychological pressure (an important début, an audition, an exam) they tend to concentrate more on technical details which they usually carry out automatically, as a matter of experience. This produces a change in routine which may compromise performance: an actor becomes nervous about his lines and freezes, a dancer loses fluency of movement, a baseball player drops the ball, and so on [Beilock and Carr, 2001]. In all these cases the natural flow of the performance is lost and the grace that goes with talent evaporates.

Whitehead [1911] made the point that, although we are constantly told to think about what we are doing – a standard prescription in school textbooks, but also in the words of wisdom proffered by eminent figures – this is actually profoundly mistaken. In fact the exact contrary is true: «Civilization advances by extending the number of important operations which we can perform without thinking about them» [Whitehead, 1911, p. 61].

Without our gut feelings it would be difficult to orient ourselves in the world and take rapid, adaptive decisions. Even shopping at the supermarket would cost us a lot in cognitive terms. For example, if we were to cast a rational look over the shelf of jams, we would be assailed by a host of contradictory thoughts, making it difficult if not impossible to choose: we would find ourselves saying «this jam is delicious», «yes, but I'm supposed to be on a diet», «I like the colours on this jar», «this is too expensive» and so on. In most cases our gut feelings and our emotions unconsciously guide our choices to a certain product. In an "emotional tug of war" [Lehrer, 2009] our choice falls on the product which fills us with the greatest pleasure.

> The experts of marketing know perfectly well that that clients in a supermarket are susceptible to the tricks of the advertiser and packer; they do not make rational choices. [...] In our society, it is the job of the influential specialty – advertisers, motivation researchers, etc. – to make choices irrational which essentially is done by coupling biological factors – conditioned reflex, unconscious drives – with symbolic values. [von Bertalanffy, 1968, pp. 115–116]

As we move along the aisles of a supermarket we carry out a very rapid visual scan of the environment. Sometimes the decision to purchase is already taken when we are still a long way away from the shelf and it is barely possible to distinguish the category of product and colours of the packaging. These stimuli act only on the surface of rationality, in that largely unexplored "cognitive unconscious" from which our decisions emerge. The emotional part of our mind reacts to even slight stimulations, such as a sound, a colour or a particular shapes. A rapid glance is enough to grasp the essence of the message, call up previous knowledge of the brand and decide to purchase. Under ten seconds suffices to complete the whole decision-making process, an interval of time which can mean success or failure for the brands in competition.

It is very interesting to observe the gap that exists between taste and sight. This can explain, for example, how one famous brand may continue to be more popular than another even when tastes would determine a different outcome. In 2004 Montague and his group carried out an experiment known as the Pepsi Challenge: 67 blindfolded participants were given two labelled glasses, one containing Coca-Cola and the other Pepsi-Cola. After drinking from each one, they had to say which they preferred. Most of the participants chose Pepsi. However, when they had to repeat the trial without the blindfold, many of those who had chosen Pepsi first time round now preferred Coca-Cola. The explanation is that the latter's logo, launched well before that of its competitor and passed down from one generation to another, was much more deeply embedded in the consumers' brain than that of Pepsi [McClure *et al.*, 2004].

It is evident that in a complex world, decision-making problems are usually characterised by the presence of a lot of information. In such classical theories as the Expected Utility Theory [von Neumann and Morgenstern, 1947] decision-making behaviour was defined as a process of integrating information which, by means of *Weighted Additive Strategies* (WADD), would always lead to the optimal choice. Traditionally the application of compensatory strategies has been used as a standard prescription for explaining rational behaviour. Nonetheless, on account of the cognitive-computational and environmental limits, in most everyday situations people do not turn to logico-formal strategies

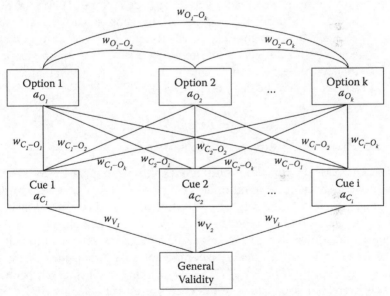

Figure 16 A general model for basic probabilistic inferences. Boxes represent nodes; lines represent links, which are all bidirectional. Connection weights can range from −1 to +1 and are labelled w. Using the iterative updating algorithm, coherence is produced in the network by changing activations [a]. The special node "General Validity" has a constant activation of +1 and is used to supply the network with energy. The indexes o and c refer to option and cue nodes, the index v refers to connections with the general validity node.
[*Source*: Glöckner, 2008, p. 313]

[Simon, 1955, 1982] but rely on automatic processes. Together with the increased interest in non compensatory, intuitive decision-making strategies, a range of other alternatives to the normative strategies have been devised. Among them there is the *Consistency-Maximizing Strategy* (CMS).

The CMS identifies three phases in the decision-making process. When confronted by a situation requiring a decision, people immediately activate the salient information available in memory to form a first mental representation of the situation. This representation can be viewed as a temporary information network. As soon as this network has been activated, automatic processes tend towards a consistent maximization in the network to reduce the incoherence between the assembled information and create a coherent representation of the situation. In the third step, people generally use this representation – in which one option usually predominates – to make a decision. As Glöckner explained:

> Using systematic simulations of the network and theoretical considerations, I derived the following predictions of CMS: (a) the choices of individuals who use CMS approximate the choices predicted by a weighted additive strategy, (b) decision times are generally short, (c) decision times increase with increasing inconsistency in the decision situation, and (d) subjective validities are changed within the decision process. [2008, p. 314]

Dual-Process Theories of Reasoning

In recent years the topic of intuition has gained in popularity and taken on increasing scientific significance [Hogarth, 2001]. We can trace the origin of studies of intuition back to Kahneman and Tversky's *Heuristics and Biases Approach*. From the 1970s they devised experiments to see how people's decisions diverged from the normative models of rationality. They showed that in many experimental tasks requiring analytic reasoning (e.g. the *Problem of the Asian Disease, see* Chapter 2), people actually tend to reason and draw inferences intuitively [Stanovich, 1999]. One possible explanation for this fact is that the concept of normative rationality does not coincide with that of adaptive rationality, or that the maximization of utility for the individual is different from that for the species [Cummins, 1996]. Starting from the study of heuristics, research into decision-making processes has seen a proliferation of approaches which go beyond the formal and deliberate cognitive processes typical of neoclassical rationality. For example, one of the lines of research which incorporate intuition in the decision-making process features dual-process theories [Chaiken and Trope, 1999; Epstein, 1994; Hammond, 1996]. From 1970 onwards these theories became particularly widespread in various areas of cognitive and social psychology, and they involved distinguishing between: automatic and controlled processes [Schneider and Shiffrin, 1977]; heuristic and systematic thinking [Chaiken, 1980]; conscious and unconscious cognition [Greenwald, 1992]; or again affect and cognition.

Analytic thought and intuition were traditionally viewed as contrasting cognitive processes, the former being characterised by precise strategies of formal and compensatory reasoning, the latter being rapid, ineffable and often unconscious in producing responses to problems. There has been an increase in dual-process theories of reasoning in recent years [Deutsch and Strack; Sloman, 1996]. Many of these dual processing models are variations of Epstein's *Cognitive Experiential Self-Theory* [1994], which featured two different modalities for knowledge, relying on experiential processes and analytic processes. Let us review some of the recent theories.

Evans and Over

This model of reasoning is based on Evans's *Heuristic Analytic Theory* [1997]. Whereas Tversky and Kahneman [1974] saw heuristics as cognitive strategies which provide shortcuts for arriving at a satisfactory choice, Evans argues that heuristic processes are pre-conscious, their function being to select the models relating to a particular decision-making problem. In 1984 he stated that normative theories of rationality do not provide a satisfactory method for assessing human reasoning, and often lead to conclusions that strike us as irrational. This problem is explained by Evans and Over [1997] with the dual-process theory postulating two distinct forms of rationality [*see* Chapter 2]. The first (System 1), also described as a heuristic, is rapid, essentially implicit, associative, pragmatic, based on previous experiences, and achieves its objectives efficiently without any conscious control. It is domain-specific, since the knowledge acquired with this system is developed in highly specialised sectors, while the mechanism of System 2 is domain-general and can be compared to a neural network in which knowledge is expressed as activations of specific units of the network and not through the activation of content-specific rules. While System 1 is a set of different types of implicit and non-conscious cognitive processes, System 2 constitutes a unitary system. Also known as analytic, it is slower, conscious, sequential and explicit. To sum up, this dual-process theory features two types of cognitive process: 1) heuristic, which generates selective models of the problem, and 2) analytic, which draws inferences from these models. The *biases* derive from the fact that in the first phase of heuristic elaboration, information which is logically significant may be ignored or even omitted.

Sloman

The dual-process theory formulated by Sloman [1996] also maintains that human cognitive processes rely on two systems. The *associative system* is based on levels of temporal contiguity and relations of resemblance acquired through personal experience. It is a rapid, automatic, concrete system, and the agent is not aware of the underlying processes but only of the end product. The *rule-based system* draws inferences by means of analytic-formal processes, and unlike in associative reasoning, the agent is aware of both the process and the end product. According to Sloman, although these two systems of reasoning lead to opposite solutions, they are not separate but act simultaneously. He refers to this simultaneous representation as "Criterion S". A classic example of the dual process is the *four-card selection task* devised by Wason [1966], see above, because the agent can be simultaneously aware of two opposite solutions to the problem, one provided by the *associative system* and the other by the *rule-based system*.

Stanovich and West

Stanovich and West [2002] combine the *Cognitive Experiential Self-Theory* [Epstein, 1994] with subsequent theories and present a unified theory based on two distinct systems of reasoning, one experiential and the other cognitive. The first provides intuitive responses to problems, and the second monitors, and if necessary corrects, these responses. In the words of the authors:

> [. . .] the most important distinction between the two systems is that they tend to lead to different types of task construals. Construals triggered by System 1 are highly contextualized, personalized and socialized. [. . .] The primacy of these mechanisms leads to what has been termed the fundamental computational bias in human cognition [. . .] – the tendency towards automatic contextualization of problems. In contrast, System 2's more controlled processes serve to decontextualize and depersonalize problems. This system is more adept at representing in terms of rules and underlying principles. It can deal with problems without social content and is not dominated by the goal of attributing intentionality nor by the search for conversational relevance. [Stanovich and West, 2000, pp. 658–659]

The primacy of System 1 prevents agents tackling a problem on the basis of its logical properties. Stanovich [1999] defines this tendency to automatically contextualise problems as *fundamental computational bias*. These differences in cognitive abilities correspond to two different types of intelligence: *analytic intelligence* (measurable by means of psychometric tests) and *interactional intelligence* (social, pragmatic intelligence). Moreover, in general people with good cognitive powers manage to avoid the temptation to base their judgements only on heuristics, and are able to solve a particular problem using the analytic processes (System 2). On the contrary, weaker cognitive powers make people more likely to rely on the heuristic processes that are immediately available in System 1.

Of the three dual-process theories, that of Stanovich and West [2000] provides the most detailed explanation of how the two systems of reasoning develop in terms of evolution. System 1 is at the service of *evolutionary rationality* and is designed to monitor and identify the naturally occurring instances of regularity in the environment. System 2, on the other hand, serves *instrumental rationality*: «System 2, while also clearly an evolutionary product, is also primarily a control System focused on the interests of the whole person. It is the primary maximizer of an individual's personal utility» [Stanovich and West, 2000, p. 656]. The variability found in problem-solving and decision-making tasks, and the discrepancy between normative and descriptive models, cannot be explained merely by the presence of errors of performance or cognitive-computational limitations. It also reflects the numerous individual differences, such as the need to finish the task as quickly as possible, the tendency to reflect thoroughly, the instinct to seek confirmation of one's own hypotheses, and so on.

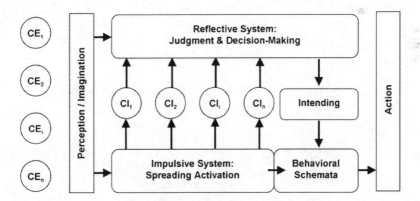

Figure 17 Schematic description of judgment and decision making in the reflective system. CE = environmental cues; CI = internal cues generated by the impulsive system (e.g., feelings, conceptual activation).
[*Source*: Deutsch and Strack, 2008, p. 40]

Reflective Impulsive Model (RIM)

In line with the underlying principles of the dual-system models, the *Reflective Impulsive Model* [Strack and Deutsch, 2004] explains behaviour as the outcome of the joint functioning of two systems of processing, each of which operates according to different principles [Figure 17]: the *reflective system* (RS) and the *impulsive system* (IS). While the former produces judgements and decisions on the basis of intentional models, the latter is activated unconsciously by means of previously acquired associations and motivational orientations [Schmidt, 1975].

The *multimodal associative memory* of the IS, which includes behavioural schemata and motivational orientations, plays a fundamental role in the decision-making process because it generates the various internal solutions in terms of affective responses and behavioural tendencies. These solutions give the individual important information about the structure of the immediate environment [Smith and DeCoster, 2000]. These *internal cues* are received by the RS and included in the formation of judgement. The operations of the RS are slower than the functions of the IS and are based on just a few, distinct symbolic representations, bringing together the various strategic action plans to achieve an objective and inhibiting the instinctive responses (such as impulses or habits). In other words, the RS provides for a flexible, higher order degree of control over decisions and actions through which immediate stimulus control can be overcome. In general the RS chooses those *cues* which (a) best satisfy the given objective and (b) are compatible with the available cognitive abilities and environmental resources.

CONCLUSIONS

Contemporary science is facing a crucial question: what is the nature of rationality? Over the last 30 years systematic analysis of human thought has come up with new and surprising evidence. In particular, cognitive neuroscience has defined a number of concrete, significant and reproducible cases which are general enough to clarify some regular features of mental processes. Of particular interest have been experimental *tasks* which can in theory be solved on the basis of precise abstract rules but which on the contrary tend to be solved in a very different way. Experimental research has shown that in their behaviour the great majority of people follow 'anomalous' spontaneous intuitions, unconsciously adopting adaptive solutions which are incompatible with normative rationality.

From an evolutionary standpoint the rapidity with which information is gathered has often been (and still is) more important than the precision of our logical inferences. In order to survive, humans have to reason on the basis of fragmentary information, within narrow time limits and restricted cognitive abilities. In the decision-making process the speed of action depends on the use of heuristic and intuitive strategies making it possible to simplify the problems, ensuring efficacy for the cognitive economy of the species. Certainly, when appropriately applied, formal logic can give acceptable results, but its processes are so slow and expensive in cognitive terms as to make it difficult to use. This surely explains why, in general, we are so inefficient at making calculations and so brilliant at estimating quantities, distances and the other variables required for survival. Moreover a lot of experimental evidence from cognitive psychology has confuted the classical hypothesis of an innate logico-formal competence, showing how the use of heuristics and intuitive decision-making strategies is part and parcel of human rationality. For this reason a realistic attempt to understand our logical capabilities requires a broad notion of logic involving the cognitive processes without confining itself to computational processes. Above all it has to recognise the component elements of fallibility. Rationality is an extremely complex ideal which we can only approach by successive approximations, as if it were almost out of our reach.

Rational choices, judgements and behaviour are not an ideal extension of spontaneous psychological norms. Nor, moreover, do the cognitive processes fall within the order of a 'small reason' or an approximate rationality. In specific situations, and above all with specific contents, the paths of rationality and of natural logic (heuristics, intuitions and so on) diverge drastically. Obviously this does not imply the existence of a conflict between spontaneous and ideal rationality. These two aspects are neither in harmony nor in conflict with each other because reason is not a faculty of our species which acts spontaneously and without effort. This recognition, derived from study and analysis of the mind carried out throughout the 20th century, should constitute the basis for a further conceptual revolution which replaces the image of an 'omniscient' mind with the more realistic image of a 'limited mind', whose procedures enable us to cope effectively with situations of uncertainty.

If it is true that rationality is conditioned by severe evolutionary limitations, the difficulty in deciding and facing up to uncertainty is not only linked to the inadequacy of the architecture of our minds but also to an 'external' model of uncertainty which does not correspond to the way in which our mind naturally functions. In brief, the difficulty is not 'inside' but 'outside' our head, that is, in the model of risk that we adopt.

As we suggested at the outset, new conceptual paradigms and new programmes for experimental research are called for in order to redefine the role of external restrictions on human action [concerning resources and available information] and reinstate the importance of the internal restrictions [limitations on calculation ability, on the capacity of memory and so on]. All this should be contemplated in a more general theoretical framework – natural logic – based not on metaphysical assumptions but on the concrete evidence provided by cognitive neurosciences. It is surely not far-fetched to imagine individuals adopting rules of behaviour enabling them on one hand to simplify their own decision-making models and on the other to coordinate with other agents so as to reduce the degree of uncertainty which characterises any complex system.

BIBLIOGRAPHY

ALCHIAN A. A. (1950) "Uncertainty revolution and economic theory". In *Journal of Political Economy*, 58 (3), pp. 211–222.

ALLAIS M. (1953) "Le comportement de l'homme rationnel devant le risque: critique des postulats et axiomes de l'école américaine". In *Econometrica*, 21, pp. 503–546.

ANDERSON N. H. (1974) "Algebraic models of perception". In Carterette E.C., Friedman, M.P. (eds.), *Handbook of Perception* (vol. 2). Academic Press, New York.

ARGOTE L. (1982) "Input uncertainty and organizational coordination in hospital emergency units". In *Administrative Science Quarterly*, 27, pp. 420–434.

ARISTOTLE (1973) *Nicomachean Ethics, In Introduction to Aristotle*, Edited with a General Introduction and Introductions to the Particular Works by Richard McKeon. Trans. W. D. Ross. The University of Chicago Press, Chicago and London.

ARKES H. R., BLUMER C. (1985) "The psychology of sunk cost". In *Organizational Behavior and Human Decision Processes*, 35 (1), pp. 124–140.

ARROW K. J. (1951) *Social Choice and Individual Values*. Wiley, New York.

ARROW K. J., HANN F. H. (1971) *General Competitive Analysis*. Holden-Day, San Francisco.

ASCH S. (1952) *Social Psychology*. Prentice-Hall, New York.

BANEY M. (1997) *The Frege Reader*. Blackwell, Oxford.

BASTICK T. (1982) *Intuition: How we think and act*. John Wiley, Chichester.

BAUMEISTER R. F. (1984) "Choking under pressure: Self-consciousness and paradoxical effects of incentives on skillful performance". In *Journal of Personality and Social Psychology*, 46, pp. 610–620.

BEACH L. R. and MITCHELL T. R. (1987) "Image theory: Principles, goals and plans in decision making". In *Acta Psychologica*, 66, (3), pp. 201–220.

BECK U. (2003) *La società cosmopolita*. il Mulino, Bologna.

BEILOCK S. L., BERENTHAL B. I., McCOY A. M., CARR T. H. (2004), "Haste does not always make waste: expertise, direction of attention, and speed versus accuracy in performing sensorimotor skills". In *Psychonomic Bulletin & Review*, 11, pp. 373–379.

BEILOCK S. L., CARR T. H. (2001) "On the fragility of skilled performance: What governs choking under pressure?" In *Journal of Experimental Psychology: General*, 130, pp. 701–725.

BELL D. E. (1982) "Regret in decision making under uncertainty". In *Operations Research*, 30 (5), pp. 961–981.

BENCIVENGA E. (1985) *Il primo libro di logica. Introduzione alla logica contemporanea*. Bollati Boringhieri, Torino.

BERNOULLI D. (1954/1738) "Exposition of a new theory on the measurement of risk". In *Econometrica*, 22 (1), pp. 23–36.

BERTALANFFY L. VON (1968) *General System Theory*. Braziller, New York.

BERTHOZ A. (2006) *Emotion and Reason: The cognitive science of decision making*. Trans. Giselle Weiss. Oxford University Press, Oxford.

BETSCH T. (2008) "The Nature of Intuition and its Neglect in Research in Judgement and Decision Making". In Plessner, H., Betsch, C., Betsch, T. (eds), *Intuition in Judgement and Decision Making*. Laurence Erlbaum Associates, New York, London.

BETSCH T. (2008) "The Nature of Intuition and its Neglect in Research in Judgement and Decision Making". In Plessner, H., Betsch, C., Betsch, T. (eds.), *Intuition in Judgement and Decision Making*. Laurence Erlbaum Associates, New York, London.

BETTMAN J. R. (1993) "The decision maker who came in from the cold". In McAlister, L., Rothschild, M. (eds.), *Advances in Consumer Research*, 10, pp. 7–11.

BONINI N., HADJICHRISTIDIS C. (2009) *Il sesto senso. Emozione e ragione nella decisione*. Il sole 24 Ore, Milano.

BOWEN J., QIU Z., LI Y. (1994) "Robust tolerance for ambiguity". In *Organizational Behavior and Human Decision Processes*, 57, (1), pp. 155–165.

BOWERS K. S., REGEHR G., BALTHAZARD C. G., PARKER K. (1990) "Intuition in the context of discovery". In *Cognitive Psychology*, 22, (1), pp. 72–110.

BRAINE M. D. S. (1978) "On the relation between the natural logic of reasoning and standard logic". In *Psychological Review*, 85 (1), pp. 1–21.

BRUNSSON N. (1985) *The Irrational Organization*. Wiley, Chichester.

BUUNK B. P., VAN DEN EIJNDEN R. J. J. M., SIERO F. W. (2002) "The double-edged sword of providing information about the prevalence of safer sex". In *Journal of Applied Social Psychology*, 32 (4), pp. 684–699.

CANARD N. F. (1801) *Principes d'économie politique*. Buisson, Paris.

CASSCELLS W., SCHOENBERGER A., GRAYBOYS T. (1978) "Interpretation by physicians of clinical laboratory results". In *New England Journal of Medicine*, 299 (18), pp. 999–1000.

CELLUCCI C. (2008) *Perché ancora la filosofia*. Laterza, Roma-Bari.

CHAIKEN S. (1980) "Heuristic versus systematic information processing and the use of source versus message cues in persuasion". In *Journal of Personality and Social Psychology*, 39, pp. 752–766.

CHAIKEN S., TROPE Y. (1999) *Dual-process Theories in Social Psychology*. Guilford, NewYork.

CUMMINS D. D. (1996) "Evidence for the innateness of deontic reasoning". In *Mind & Language*, 11, pp. 160-190.

CURLEY S. P., YATES J. F., ABRAMS R.A. (1986) "Psychological sources of ambiguity avoidance". In *Organizational Behavior and Human Decision Processes*, 38 (2), pp. 643–669.

DAWES R. M. (1979) "The robust beauty of improper linear models in decision making". In *American Psychologist*, 34, pp. 571–582.

DAWKINS R. (1989) *The Selfish Gene*. Oxford University Press, Oxford.

DE FINETTI B. (1970) *Teoria delle probabilità*. Einaudi, Torino.

DESCARTES R. (1637) *Discours de la Méthode*. Trans. John Cottingham, Robert Stoothoff and Dugald Murdoch (1985), *Discourse on the Method in The Philosophical Writings of Descartes*, Vol. 1. Cambridge University Press, Cambridge.

DESTENO D., PETTY R. E. WEGENER D. T., RUCKER D. D. (2000) "Beyond valence in the perception of likelihood: the role of emotion specificity". In *Journal of Personality and Social Psychology*, 78 (3), pp. 397-416.

DEUTSCH R., STRACK F. (2008) Variants of Judgment and Decision Making. The Perspective of the Reflective-Impulsive Model. In Plessner H., Betsch C., Betsch T. (eds.), *Intuition in Judgement and Decision Making*. Laurence Erlbaum Associates, New York, London.

DI NUOVO S. (2008) *Misurare la mente: i testi cognitivi e di personalità*. Laterza, Roma.

DOLINSKY D., GROMSKY W., ZAWINSZA E. (1986) "Unrealistic pessimism". In *Journal of Social Psychology*, 127 (5), pp. 511–516.

DRIVER M. J., BROUSSEAU K. R., HUNSAKER P. L. (1990) *The Dynamic Decision Maker*. Harper and Row Publishers, New York.

EDDY D. M. (1982) "Probabilistic reasoning in clinical medicine: problems and opportunities". In Kahneman, D., Slovic, P., Tversky, A. (eds.), *Judgment under Uncertainty: Heuristics and biases*. Cambridge University Press, Cambridge.

EDGEWORTH F. Y. (1881) *Mathematical Psychics: Essays on the application of mathematics to the moral sciences*. Kegan Paul & Co, London.

EKMAN P. (1992) "An Argument for the Basic Emotions". In *Cognition and Emotion*, 6 (3–4), pp. 169–200.

ELLSBERG D. (1961) "Risk, ambiguity, and the Savage axioms". In *Quarterly Journal of Economics*, 75, pp. 643–669.

EPSTEIN S. (1991) "Cognitive-experiental self-theory: An integrative theory of personality". In R. Curtis (ed.), *The Relational Self: Convergences in psychoanalysis and social psychology*. Guilford, New York.

EPSTEIN S. (1994) "Integration of the cognitive and the psychodynamic unconscious". In *American Psychologist*, 49, pp. 709–724.

EPSTEIN S., PACINI R., DENES-RAJ V., HEINER H. (1996) "Individual difference in intuitive-experiential and analytical-rational thinking styles". In *Journal of Personality and Social Psychology*, 71, pp. 390–405.

ERICSSON K., PATEL V., KINTSCH W. (2000) "How experts'adaptations to representative task demands account for the expertise effect in memory recall: Comment on Vincente and Wang" (1998). In *Psychological Review*, 107 (3), pp. 578–592.

EVANS J., OVER D. (1997) "Rationality in reasoning: The problem of deductive competence". In *Cahiers de psychologie cognitive*, 16, pp. 102–106.

FISCHHOFF B., GONZALEZ R. M., LERNER J. S., SMALL D. A. (2005) "Evolving judgments of terror risks: foresight, hindsight, and emotions". In *Journal of Experimental Psychology*, 11 (2), pp. 124–139.

FISHBURN P. C. (1974) "Lexicographic Orders, Utilities and Decision Rules: A Survey". In *Management Science*, 20 (11), pp. 1442–1471.

FRANKLIN B. (Passy, 8 aprile 1779) *Letter to Jonathan Williams* (1907). In *The Writings of Benjamin Franklin*, vol. 7. Macmillan, New York.

FREGE G. (1879) *Begriffsschrift; eine der arithmetischen nachgebildete Formelsprache des reines Denkens.* Nebert, Halle.

FREGE G. (1884) *Die Grundlagen der Arithmetik*, Wilhel Koebner, Breslau (GLA).

FREGE G. (1906) "Kurze Übersicht meiner logischen Leheren". In Hermes, H., Kambartel, F., Kaulbach, F. (eds.), *Nachgelassene Schrifte und Wisseschaftlicher Briefwechsel*. Meiner Verlag, Hamburg.

FREGE G. (1969) *Nachgelassene Schriften*, ed. by Hermes H., Kambartel F., Thiel C., Veraart A. Meiner, Hamburg.

FRIEDMAN M. (1953) "The methodology of positive economics". In Friedman, M. (ed.), *Essays in Positive Economics*. University of Chicago Press, Chicago.

FRIJDA N. H., MANSTEAD A. S. R., BEM S. (2000) *Emotions and beliefs: how feelings influence thoughts*. Cambridge University Press, Cambridge.

FUSTER J. (1997) "Network Memory". In *Trends in Neuroscience*, 20 (10), pp. 451–459.

GALBRAITH J. (1973) *Designing Complex Organizations*. Addison Wesley, Reading, Mass.

GIGERENZER G. (1997) *Bounded Rationality: Models of Fast and Frugal Inference*, Max Planck Institute for Human Development, Berlin.

GIGERENZER G. (2001) "The adaptive toolbox". In Gigerenzer, G., Selten, R. (eds.), *Bounded Rationality: The Adaptive Toolbox*. MIT Press, Cambridge, Mass.

GIGERENZER G. (2002) *Reckoning with Risk: Learning to live with uncertainty*. Allen Lane/Penguin, London.

GIGERENZER G. (2003) *Quando i numeri ingannano*. Cortina, Milano.

GIGERENZER G. (2005) "I think therefore I err". In *Social Research*, 71 (1), pp. 1–24.

GIGERENZER G. (2007) *Gut Feelings: The intelligence of the unconscious*. Viking, New York.

GIGERENZER G. (2008) *Rationaity for Mortals: How people cope with uncertainty*. Oxford University Press, New York.

GIGERENZER G., GOLDSTEIN D. G. (1996) "Reasoning the fast and frugal way: Models of bounded rationality". In *Psychological Review*, 103 (4), pp. 650–669.

GIGERENZER G., HOFFRAGE U. (1995) "How to improve Bayesian reasoning without instruction: Frequency formats". In *Psychological Review*, 102 (4), pp. 684–704.

GIGERENZER G., SWIJTINK Z., PORTER T., DASTON L., BEATTY J., KRÜGER L. (1989) *The Empire of Chance: How probability changed science and everyday life*. Cambridge University Press, Cambridge.

GIGERENZER G., TODD P. M. (1999) "Fast and Frugal Heuristics: The Adaptive Toolbox". In Gigerenzer, G., Todd, P. M., Abc Research Group (eds.), *Simple Heuristics That Make Us Smart*. Oxford University Press, New York; Oxford.

GILHOOLY K. J. (1990) "Cognitive psychology and medical diagnosis". In *Applied Cognitive Psychology*, 4 (4), pp. 261–272.

GILOVICH T., GRIFFIN D., KAHNEMAN D. (2002) (eds.), *The Psychology of Intuitive Judgment: Heuristics and biases*. Cambridge University Press, Cambridge.

GIROTTO V. (1994) *Il ragionamento*. Il Mulino, Bologna.

GLASER M., WEBER M. (2005) "Overconfidence and trading volume". In *Working Paper*, University of Mannheim.

GLÖCKNER A. (2008) "Does Intuition Beat Fast and Frugal Heuristics? A Systematic Empirical Analysis". In Plessner, H., Betsch, C., Betsch, T. (eds.), *Intuition in Judgement and Decision Making*. Laurence Erlbaum Associates, New York, London.

GOLDSTEIN D.G., GIGERENZER G. (2002) "Models of ecological rationality: the recognition heuristic". In *Psychological Review*, 109 (1), pp. 75–90.

GOLEMAN D. (1996) *Emotional Intelligence: Why it can matter more than IQ*. Bloomsbury, London.

GOULD S. J. (1992) *Bully for Brontosaurus: Further reflections in natural history*. Penguin Books, London.

GRANDORI A. (1984) "A prescriptive contingency view of organizational decision making". In *Administrative Science Quarterly*, 29, pp. 192–209.

GREENWALD A. G. (1992) "New Look 3: Reclaiming unconscious cognition". In *American Psychologist*, 47, 766–779.

HAMILTON D. L., GIFFORD R. K. (1976) "Illusory Correlation in Interpersonal Perception: A cognitive bases of stereotypic judgments". In *Journal of Experimental and Social Psychology*, 12 (4), pp. 136–149.

HAMMOND K. R. (1996) *Human Judgment and Social Policy: Incredible uncertainty, inevitable error, unavoidable justice*. Oxford University Press, New York.

HARMON-JONES E. (2003) "Clarifying the emotive functions of

asymmetrical frontal cortical activity". In *Psychophysiology*, 40 (6), pp. 838–848.

HASTIE R., DAWES R. M. (2001) *Rational Choice in an Uncertain World: The psychology of judgment and decision making*. Sage, Thousand Oaks.

HAYEK F. A. (1937) "Economics and knowledge". In *Economica*, 4 (13), pp. 96–105. Reprinted in Hayek, F. A. (1949), *Individualism and Economic Order*. Routledge & Sons, London.

HAYEK F. A. (1952) *The Sensory Order. An inquiry into the foundations of theoretical psychology*. Routledge & Kegan Paul, London.

HAYEK F. A. (1967) *Studies in Philosophy, Politics and Economics*. Routledge & Kegan Paul, London.

HAYEK F. A. (1973) *Law, Legislation and Liberty: A new statement of the liberal principles of justice and political economy*. Routledge & Kegan Paul,London.

HAYEK F. A. (1982) "The Sensory Order after 25 years". In Walter B. Weimer and David S. Palermo (eds.), *Cognition and the Symbolic Processes*, vol. 2. Hillsdale, New York.

HAYEK F. A. (1994) *Hayek on Hayek: An autobiographical dialogue*. Edited by Kresge S. and Wenar L. Chicago, University of Chicago Press, Routledge, London.

HEINER R. A. (1983) "The origin of predictable bahavior". In *American Economic Review*, 4, pp. 560–595.

HELMHOLTZ H. VON (1967) "Trattato sull'ottica fisiologica". In *Opere scelte*. UTET, Torino.

HENDRICKX L., VLEK C. (1991) "Perceived control nature of risk information and risk taking. An experimental test of a simple taxonomy of uncertainty". In *Journal of Behavioral Decision Making*, 4 (4), pp. 235–247.

HEY J. D. (1979) *Uncertainty in Microeconomics*. Martin Robertson, Oxford.

HODGSON G. H. (1991) *Economia e istituzioni*. Otium Edizioni, Ancona.

HOFFRAGE U., GIGERENZER G. (1998) "Using natural frequencies to improve diagnostic inferences". In *Academic Medicine*, 73 (5), pp. 538–540.

HOGARTH R. (2001) *Educating Intuition*. The University of Chicago Press, Chicago.

HOGARTH R. M. (1987) *Judgement and Choice: The psychology of decision*. Wiley, New York.

HOGART R. M., REDER M. W. (1986) *Rational Choice: The contrast between economics and psychology*. The University of Chicago Press, Chicago.

INGRAO B., ISRAEL G. (1990) *The invisible hand: economic equilibrium in the history of science*. Cambridge, Mass., London.

INHELDER B., PIAGET J. (1955) *De la logique de l'enfant à la logique de l'adolescent*. Presses Universitaires de France, Paris.

ISRAEL G. (2004) *La macchina vivente. Contro le visioni meccanicistiche dell'uomo*. Bollati Boringhieri, Turin.

JAMES, W. (1950) *The Principles of Psychology*, vol. II. New York: Dover Publications.

JEVONS W. S. (1871) *The Theory of Political Economy*. Macmillan, London.

JOHNSON E. J., PAYNE J. W. (1985) "Effort and accuracy in choice". In *Management Science*, 31 (4), pp. 394–414.

JOHNSON-LAIRD P. N. (1983) *Mental Models*. Harvard University Press, Cambridge, Mass.

KAHNEMAN D., FREDERICK S. (2002) "Representativeness revisited: Attribute substitution in intuitive judgment". In Gilovich T., Griffin D. and Kahneman D. (eds.), *Heuristics and Biases: The psychology of intuitive judgment*. Cambridge University Press, Cambridge.

KAHNEMAN D., FREDERICK S. (2005) "A model of heuristic judgment". In Holyoak K.J. and Morrison R.G. (eds.), *The Cambridge Handbook of Thinking and Reasoning*. Cambridge University Press, New York.

KAHNEMAN D., KNETSCH J., THALER R. (1991) "The endowment effect, loss aversion, and status quo bias". In *Journal of Economic Perspectives*, 5, pp. 193–206.

KAHNEMAN D., SLOVIC P., TVERSKY A. (1982) *Judgment under Uncertainty: Heuristics and biases*. Cambridge University Press, New York.

KAHNEMAN D., TVERSKY A. (1973) "On the psychology of prediction". In *Psychological Review*, 80, pp. 237–251.

KAHNEMAN D., TVERSKY A. (1979) "Prospect theory: an analysis of decisions under risk". In *Econometrica*, 47, pp. 313–327.

KAHNEMAN D., TVERSKY A. (1984) "Choices, values and frames". In *American Psychologist*, 39, pp. 341–350.

KANIZSA G. (1979) *Organization in Vision: Essays on gestalt perception*. Praeger, New York.

KANT I. (1919) *Critica della ragion pura*. Laterza, Bari.

KAPLAN S., GARRICK J. B. (1981) "On the quantitative definition of risk". In *Risk Analysis*, 1 (1), pp. 11–27.

KASPAROV G. K. (2007) *How Life Imitates Chess*. Bloomsbury USA, New York.

KEYNES J. M. (1952) *A Treatise on Probability*. Macmillan, London.

KLEIN G. A. (1993) "Recognition-primed decisions". In W. B. Rouse (ed.), *Advances in Man-Machine Systems Research*. JAI Press, Greenwich.

KLEIN G. A. (1998) *Sources of Power: How people make decisions*. MIT Press, Cambridge, Mass.

KLEIN G. A., CALDERWOOD R. (1991) "Decision Model: some lessons from the field". In *IEEE Transactions on Systems Man and Cybernetics*, 21 (5), pp. 1018–1026.

KLEIN G. A., CRANDALL B. W. (1995) "The role of mental simulation in naturalistic decision making". In Hancock P., Flach J., Caird J., Vicente K. (eds.), *Local Applications of the Ecological Approach to Human-Machine Systems*. Lawrence Erlbaum, Hillsdale.

KNIGHT F. (1921) *Risk, Uncertainty and Profit*. Houghton Mifflin, Boston and New York.

KOYRÉ A. (1968) *Newtonian Studies*. University of Chicago Press, Chicago.

KUIPERS B., MOSKOWITZ A. J., KASSIRER J. P. (1988) "Critical decisions under untertainty: Representation and structure". In *Cognitive Science*, 12 (2), pp. 177–210.

LAIBSON D., ZECKHAUSER R. (1999) "Amos Tversky and the Ascent of Behavioral Economics". In *Theory and Decision*, 16 (1), pp. 7–47.

LANGER E. J. (1975) "The illusion of control". In *Journal of Personality and Social Psychology*, 32 (2), pp. 311–328.

LAPLACE P. S. (1825) *Essai philosophique des probabilités*. Bachelier, Paris. Tr. Eng. (1995), *Philosophical Essay on Probabilities*. Springer-Verlag, New York.

LAZARUS R. S. (1991) *Emotion and Adaptation*. Oxford University Press, New York.

LEHRER J. (2009) *How we decide*. Houghton Mifflin Harcourt, Boston; New York.

LEIBNIZ G. W. (1890) *Philosophische Schriften*, Vol. VII, Berlin.

LEMMON E. J. (2008) *Elementi di Logica*. Laterza, Roma-Bari.

LERNER J. S., KELTNER D. (2000) "Beyond valence: Toward a model of emotion-specific influences on judgment and choice". In *Cognition and Emotion*, 4 (4), pp. 473–493.

LETWIN S. R., REYNOLDS N. B. (2005) *On the History of the Idea of Law*. Cambridge University press, Cambridge.

LIPSHITZ R., KLEIN G., ORASANU G., SALAS E. (2001) "Taking stock of Naturalistic Decision Making". In *Journal of Behavioral Decision Making*, 14 (5), pp. 331–352.

LIPSHITZ R., STRAUSS O. (1997) "Coping with uncertainty: A naturalistic decision making analysis". In *Organizational Behavior and Human Decision Processes*, 69 (2), pp. 149–163.

LOCKE J. (1690) *An Essay Concerning Human Understanding*. Basset, London.

LOEWENSTEIN G., WEBER E., HSEE C., WELCH N. (2001) "Risk as Feelings". In *Psychological Bulletin*, 127 (2), pp. 267–286.

LOOMS G., SUGDEN R. (1982) "Regret theory: an alternative theory of rational choice under uncertainty". In *Economic Journal*, 92 (368), pp. 805–824.

LOPES L. L. (1997) "Between Hope and Fear: The Psychology of Risk". In Goldstein W. M., Hogarth R.M. (eds.), *Research on Judgment and Decision Making*. Cambridge University Press, New York.

LUCAS E. R. (1981) *Studies in Business Cycle Theory*. MIT Press, Cambridge, Mass.

LUPTON D. (2003) *Il rischio. Percezione, simboli, culture*. Il Mulino, Bologna.

MACLEOD C., CAMPBELL L. (1992) "Memory Accessibily and Probability Judgments: An experimental evaluation of the availability heuristic". In *Journal of Personality and Social Psychology*, 63, pp. 890–902.

MACGREGOR D.G., SLOVIC P., DREMAN D., BERRY M. (2000) "Imagery, affect and financial judgment". In *The Journal of Psychology and Financial Markets*, 1, pp. 104–110.

MALDONATO M. (2010) *Decision Making: Towards an Evolutionary Psychology of Rationality*. Sussex Academic Press, Brighton; Portland; Toronto.

MALDONATO M., DELL'ORCO S. (2010) "Toward an Evolutionary Theory of Rationality". In *World Futures*, 66 (2), pp. 103–123.

MANDEVILLE B. (1714) *The Fable of the Bees. Or: private vices, publick benefits*, Oxfor Arms in Warwick Lane.

MANKTELOW K., OVER D. (1990) *Inference and Understanding*. Routledge, London.

MARCH J. G. (1994) *A Primer on Decision Making: How decisions happen*. The Free Press, New York.

MARCH J. G., SIMON H. A. (1958) *Organizations*. John Wiley and Sons, New York.

MARSCHAK J. e RADNER R. (1972) *Economic Theory of Teams*. Yale University press, New Haven.

McBEATH M. K., SHAFFER D. M., MORGAN S. E., SUGAR T. G. (2002) *Lack of Conscious Awareness of How We Navigate to Catch Baseballs*, University of Arizona, Tucson.

McCLURE S. M., LI J., TOMLIN D., CYPERT K. S., MONTAGUE L. M., MONTAGUE P. R. (2004) "Neural Correlates of behavioral preference for culturally familiar drinks". In *Neuron*, 44, pp. 167–202.

McFADDEN D. (2005) "Razionalità per economisti?". In Motterlini M., Piattelli Palmarini M. (eds.), *Critica della ragione economica. Tre saggi: Kahneman, McFadden, Smith*. Il Saggiatore, Milano.

MENGER C. (1871) *Grundsätze der Volkswirthschaftslehre*. Wilhelm Braumüller, Vienna.

MIROWSKI P. (1989) *More Heat than Light: Economics as social physics, physics as nature's economics*. Cambridge University Press, New York.

MONTAGUE P. R. (2006) *Why Choose this Book? How we make decisions*. Dutton, Toronto.

MULLAINATHAN S., THALER R. H (2000) "Behavioral economics". In *National Bureau of Economic Research (NBER)*, Working Paper 7948.

NEUMANN J. VON, MORGENSTERN O. (1947) *Theory of Games and Economic Behavior*. Princeton University Press, Princeton.

NISBETT R. E., ROSS L. (1980) *Human Inference: Strategies and shortcomings of social judgment*. Prentice-Hall, Englewood Cliffs.

NOREM J. K., CANTOR N. (1986) "Defensive pessimism: Harnessing anxiety as motivation". In *Journal of Personality and Social Psychology*, 51 (6), pp. 1208–1217.

NOZICK R. (1993) *The Nature of Rationality*. Princeton University Press, Princeton, NJ.

OLIVERIO A. (2007) *Strategie della scelta. Introduzione alla teoria della decisione*. Laterza, Roma-Bari.

OTTEN W., VAN DER PLIGT J. (1996) "Context effects in the

measurement of comparative optimism in probability judgments". In *Journal of Social and Clinical Psychology*, 15 (1), pp. 80–101.

PALLER K. A. (2001) *Neurocognitive Foundations of Human Memory*. In Medin D. L. (ed.), *The Psychology of Learning and Motivation*. Academic Press, San Diego.

PANTALEONI M. (1889) *Principii di economia pura*. Barbera, Firenze.

PATEL V. L., GROEN G. J. (1991) "The general and specific nature of medical expertise: A critical look". In Ericsson K. A., Smith J. (eds.), *Toward a General Theory of Expertise: Prospects and limits*. Cambridge University Press, Cambridge.

PAYNE J. W. (1976) "Task complexity and contingent processing in decision making: An information search and protocol analysis". In *Organizational Behavior and Human Performance*, 16, pp. 366–387.

PAYNE J. W., BETTMAN J.R., JOHNSON E.J. (1993) *The Adaptive Decision Maker*. Cambridge University Press, Cambridge.

POLANYI M. (1951) *The Logic of Liberty*. Routledge and Kegan, London.

PUGH D. S., HICKSON D. J. (2007) *Great Writers on Organizations*. Ashgate, Aldershot.

QUADREL M. J., FISHHOFF B., DORIS W. (1993) "Adolescent (In)vulnerability". In *American Psychologist*, 48 (2), pp. 102–116.

RAMO P. (de la Ramée, Pierre) (1964a) "Dialecticae institutiones". In Ramo P. (ed.), *Dialecticae institutiones. Aristotelicae animadversiones*. F. Frommann, Stuttgart.

RAMO P. (de la Ramée, Pierre) (1964b) "Aristotelicae animadversiones". In Ramo P. (ed.), *Dialecticae institutiones. Aristotelicae animadversiones*. F. Frommann, Stuttgart.

RICHARDSON R. C. (1998) "Heuristics and satisficing". In Bechtel W., Graham, G. (eds.), *A Companion to Cognitive Science*. Blackwell Publishers, Oxford.

RIZZELLO S. (1997) *L'economia della mente*. Laterza, Roma-Bari.

ROBBINS L. (1932) *An Essay on the Nature and Significance of Economic Science*. Macmillan, London.

RUMIATI R. (2000) *Decidere*. Il Mulino, Bologna.

RUMIATI R., BONINI N. (1992) "Psicologia della decisione e decisioni economiche". In *Sistemi Intelligenti*, 4, pp. 357–378.

RUSSO J. E., DOSHER B. A. (1983) "Strategies for multiattribute binary choice". In *Journal of Experimental Psychology: Learning, Memory, & Cognition*, 9, pp. 676–696.

SACKETT D. L., RICHARDSON W. S., ROSENBERG W., HAYNES R. B. (1997) *Evidence-Based Medicine. How to practice and teach EBM*. Churchill Livingstone, New York.

SAVADORI L., RUMIATI R. (1996) "Percezione del rischio negli adolescenti italiani". In *Giornale Italiano di Psicologia*, 23, pp. 85–106.

SAVADORI L., RUMIATI R. (2005) *Nuovi rischi, vecchie paure*. Il Mulino, Bologna.

SAVAGE L. J. (1954) *The Foundations of Statistics*. John Wiley and Sons, New York.

SCHNEIDER W., SHIFFRIN R. M. (1977) "Controlled and automatic human information processing: I. Detection, search, and attention". In *Psychological Review*, 84, pp. 1–66.

SCHEIER M. F., CARVER C. S. (1987) "Dispositional optimism and physical well-being: The influence of generalized outcome expectances on health". In *Journal of Personality*, 55, (2), pp. 169–210.

SCHMIDT R. A. (1975) "A schema theory of discrete motor skill learning". In *Psychological Review*, 82, pp. 225–260.

SCHUMETER J. A. (1939) *Business Cycles*. McGraw Hill, New York.

SCHWARTZ J. H., KANDEL E. R., JASSEL T. M. (1991) *Principles of neural science*. Prentice-Hall International, London.

SCHWARZ N. (1990) "Feelings as information: informational and motivational functions of affective states". In Sorrentino R. M., Higgins E.T. (eds.), *Handbook of Motivation and Cognition: Foundations of social behavior*. Guilford Press, New York.

SCHWARZ N., VAUGHN L. A. (2002) "The availability heuristic revisited: Recalled content and ease of recall as information". In Gilovich T., Griffin D. and Kahneman D. (eds.), *The Psychology of Intuitive Judgment: Heuristics and biases*. Cambridge University Press, Cambridge, England.

SCOTT S. G., BRUCE R. A. (1995). "Decision making style: the development of a new measure". In *Educational and Psychological Measurement*, 55, pp. 818–831.

SELTEN R. (1998) "Aspiration adaptation theory". In *Journal of Mathematical Psychology*, 42, pp. 191–214.

SHAFER G., PEARL J. (1990) *Readings in Uncertain Reasoning*. Morgan Kauffman, San Matteo.

SHEFRIN H., THALER R. H. (1992) Mental accounting, saving, and self-control. In Lowenstein G., Elster J. (eds.), *Choice over Time*. Russell Sage Foundation, New York, pp. 287–330.

SIMON H. A (1957) *Administrative Behavior: A study of decision-making process in administrative organization*, 2nd edition. Macmillan, New York.

SIMON H. A. (1955) "A Behavioral Model of Rational Choice". In *Quarterly Journal of Economics*, 69, (1), pp. 99–118.

SIMON H. A. (1957) *Administrative Behavior: A study of decision-making process in administrative organization*. 2nd edition. Macmillan, New York.

SIMON H. A. (1958), "The Role of Expectations in an Adaptive or Behavioristic Model". In Bowman M. J. (ed.), *Expectations, Uncertainty and Business Behavior*. Social Sciences Research Council, New York.

SIMON H. A. (1978) "Information-processing theory of human problem solving". In Estes, W. K. (ed.), *Handbook of Learning and Cognitive Processes*. Erlbaum, Hillsdale, New York.

SIMON H. A. (1979) "Rational decision making in business organizations" (Nobel Lecture, Stockholm, 1978) In *American Economic Review*, 69, pp. 493–512.

SIMON H. A. (1983) "Alternative visions of rationality". In Moser, P. K. (ed.), *Rationality in Action: Contemporary approaches*. Cambridge University Press.

SIMON H. A. (1983) *Reason in Human Affairs*. Stanford University Press, Stanford, California.

SIMON H. A. (1985) *Causalità, razionalità, organizzazione*. Il Mulino, Bologna.

SIMON H. A. (1997) *Models of Bounded Rationality*, vol. 3. MIT Press, Boston.

SIMONSON I. (1992) "The influence of anticipating regret and responsibility on purchase decisions". In *Journal of Consumer Research*, 19 (1), pp. 105–118.

SLOMAN S. A. (1996) "The empirical case for two systems of reasoning". In *Psychological Bulletin*, 119, pp. 3–22.

SLOVIC P. (1972) "Psychological study of human judgment: implications for investment decision making". In *The Journal of Finance*, 27 (4), pp. 779–799.

SLOVIC P. (1987) "Perception of Risk". In *Science*, 236 (4799), pp. 280–285.

SLOVIC P. (2000) *The Perception of Risk*. Earthscan, London.

SLOVIC P., FISCHHOFF B., LICHTENSTEIN S. (1976) "Cognitive Processes and societal risk taking". In Carroll J.S., Payne, J.W. (eds.), *Cognition and Social Behavior*. Erlbaum, Hillsdale.

SLOVIC P., FISCHHOFF B., LICHTENSTEIN S. (1980) "Facts and fears: Understanding perceived risk". In Schwing, R., Albers Jr. W.A. (eds) *Societal Risk Assessment: How safe is safe enough?* Plenum Press, New York.

SLOVIC P., LAYMAN M., KRAUS N., FLYNN J., CHALMERS J., GESELL G. (1991) "Perceived risk, stigma and potential economic impacts of a high level nuclear waste repository in Nevada". In *Risk Analysis*, 11, pp. 683– 696.

SMITH A. (1759) *The Theory of Moral Sentiments*. Printed for Millar A., Kincaid A. and Bell J., London.

SMITH A. (1776) *An inquiry into the causes of the wealth of nations*. Edinburgh.

SMITH C. A., ELLSWORTH P. C. (1985) "Patterns of cognitive appraisal in emotion". In *Journal of Personality and Social Psychology*, 48, pp. 813–838.

SMITH E. R., DeCOSTER J. (2000) "Dual process models in social and cognitive psychology: Conceptual integration and links to underlying memory systems". In *Personality and Social Psychology Review*, 4, pp. 108–131.

SMITHSON M. (1989) *Ignorance and Uncertainty: Emerging paradigms*. Springer Verlag, New York.

STANOVICH K. E. (1999) *Who is rational? Studies of individual differences in reasoning*. Erlbaum, Hillsdale.

STANOVICH K. E., WEST R. F. (2000) "Individual differences in reasoning: Implications for the rationality debate". In *Behavioral and Brain Sciences*, 23, pp. 645–665.

STANOVICH K. E., WEST R. F. (2002) "Individual differences in reasoning: Implications for the rationality debate?" In T. Gilovich, D. Griffin, D. Kahneman (eds.), *Heuristics and Biases: The psychology of intuitive judgment*. Cambridge University Press, New York.

STARR C. (1969) "Social benefit versus technological risk. What is our society willing to pay for safety?". In *Science*, 165 (19), pp. 1232–1238.

STARR C. e WHIPPLE C. (1980) "Risk of Risk Decision". In *Science*, 208 (4448), pp. 1114–1119.

STIGLER G. (1961) "The economics of information". In *Journal of Political Economy*, 69, pp. 213–25.

THALER R. H. (1980) "Towards a positive theory of consumer choice". In *Journal of Economic Behavior and Organization*, 1 (1), pp. 39–60.

THALER R. H. (1999) "Mental accounting matters". In *Journal of Behavioral Decision Making*, 12, pp. 183–206.

THOMPSON J. (1967) *Organizations in Action*. McGraw, Hill, New York.

TIETZ R. (1992) "Semi-normative theories based on bounded rationality". In *Journal of Economic Psychology*, 13 (2), pp. 297–314.

TODD P. M., GIGERENZER G. (2000) "Précis of simple heuristics that make us smart". In *Behavioral and Brain Sciences*, 23 (5), pp. 727–780.

TSEBELIS G. (1990) *Nested Games: Rational choice in comparative politics*. University of California, Berkeley.

TVERSKY (1972) "Elimination by aspects: A Theory of Choice". In *Psychological Review*, 79 (4), pp. 281–299.

TVERSKY A. (1969) "Intransitivity of preferences". In *Psychological Review*, 76 (1), pp. 31–48.

TVERSKY A., KAHNEMAN D. (1974) "Judgment under uncertainty: heuristics and biases". In *Science*, 185 (4157), pp. 1124–1131.

TVERSKY A., KAHNEMAN D. (1981) "The framing of decisions and the psychology of choice". In *Science*, 211 (4481), pp. 453–458.

TVERSKY A., KAHNEMAN D. (1982) "Availability: a heuristic for judging frequency and probability". In Kahneman, D., Slovic, P. and Tversky, A. (eds.), *Judgment under Uncertainty: Heuristics and Biases*. Cambridge University Press, Cambridge.

TVERSKY A., KAHNEMAN D. (1983) "Extensional Versus Intuitive Reasoning: The Conjunction Fallacy in Probability Judgment". In *Psychological Review*, 90, (4), pp. 293–315.

TVERSKY A., SATTAH S., SLOVIC P. (1988) "Contingent weighting in judgment and choice". In *Psychological Review*, 95, pp. 371–384.

WALRAS A. (1831) *De la nature de la richesse et de l'origine de la valeur*. Johanneau, Paris.

WALRAS L. (1874) *Elements of pure economics: or the theory of social wealth*. Jaffe, W., George Allen and Unwin, London.

WALRAS L. (1900) *Eleménts d'économie politique pure ou théorie de la richesse sociale*, IV ed. Rouge, Lausanne, Pichon, Paris.

WALRAS L. (1936) *Étude d'économie sociale: théorie de la répartition de la richesse sociale*. F. Pichon, Paris.

WASON P. C. (1960) "On the failure to eliminate hypotheses in a conceptual task". In *Quarterly Journal of Experimental Psychology*, 12 (3), pp. 129–140.

WASON P. C. (1960) "On the failure to eliminate hypotheses in a conceptual task". In *Quarterly Journal of Experimental Psychology*, 12 (3), pp. 129–140.

WEBER M. (1954) *Economy and Society*. Harvard University Press, Cambridge, Mass.

WEICK K. E. (1995) *Sensemaking in Organizations*. Sage Publications, Thousand Oaks.

WEINSTEIN N. D. (1980) "Unrealistic optimism about future life events". In *Journal of Personality and Social Psychology*, 39 (5), pp. 806–820.

WHITEHEAD A. N. (1911) *An Introduction to Mathematics*. Williams and Norgate, London.

WUNDT W. (1912) *An Introduction to Psychology*. George Allen, London.

YATES J. F., STONE E. R. (1992) "The risk construct". In Yates, J. F. (ed.), *Risk-taking behaviour*. John Wiley, Chichester.

YATES J. F., STONE E. R. (1992) *The risk construct*. In Yates, J. F. (ed.), *Risk-taking behaviour*. John Wiley, Chichester.

ZAJONC R. B. (1980) "Feeling and Thinking: Preference Needs no Inference". In *American Psychologist*, 35, pp. 151–175.

ZIPF G. K. (1949) *Human behavior and the principle of least effort*. Addison Wesley Press, Cambridge.

INDEX